Battleground Europe

THE CHANNEL PORTS

110632223

CALAIS - 1940

A Fight to the Finish

Other guides in the Second World War Battleground Europe Series:

Pegasus Bridge/Merville Battery *by* Carl Shilleto
Gold Beach *by* Christopher Dunphie & Garry Johnson
Omaha Beach *by* Tim Kilvert-Jones
Battle of the Bulge - St Vith *by* Michael Tolhurst
Dunkirk *by* Patrick Wilson
March of Das Reich to Normandy *by* Philip Vickers
Hill 112 *by* Tim Saunders

Previous page: An abandoned British Cruiser tank MkIII belonging to HQ Squadron 3RTR seen here along with other abandoned vehicles near the Gare Maritime, Calais.

With the continued expansion of the Battleground Series a **Battleground Series Club** has been formed to benefit the reader. The purpose of the Club is to keep members informed of new titles and key developments by way of a quarterly newsletter, and to offer many other reader-benefits. Membership is FREE and by registering an interest you can help us predict print runs and thus maintain prices at their present levels. Please call the office on telephone no. 01226 734555, or send your name and address along with a request for more information to:
Battleground Series Club
Pen & Sword Books Ltd, 47 Church Street, Barnsley, South Yorkshire, S70 2AS

Battleground Europe
THE CHANNEL PORTS

CALAIS - 1940
A FIGHT TO THE FINISH

Jon Cooksey

LEO COOPER

COMBINED PUBLISHING
Pennsylvania

This book is dedicated to my mother and to the memory of my father,
Clifton Cooksey 1920-1989

Published by
LEO COOPER
an imprint of
Pen & Sword Books Limited
47 Church Street, Barnsley, South Yorkshire S70 2AS

Copyright © Jon Cooksey 2000

ISBN 0 85052 647 7

A CIP record of this book is available
from the British Library

Printed by Redwood Books Limited
Trowbridge, Wiltshire

*For up-to-date information on other titles produced under the Leo Cooper
imprint, please telephone or write to:*
Pen & Sword Books Ltd, FREEPOST SF5, 47 Church Street
Barnsley, South Yorkshire S70 2BR
Telephone 01226 734222

Published under license in the United States of America by

COMBINED PUBLISHING

ISBN 1-58097-011-7

For information, address:
COMBINED PUBLISHING
P.O. Box 307
Conshohocken, PA 19428
E-Mail: combined@dca.net
Web: www.combinedpublishing.com
Orders: 1-800-418-6065

*Cataloging in Publication Data available from the Library of
Congress*

CONTENTS

Calais after its capture by the Germans, 26 May 1940.

FOREWORD
by
BRIGADIER
GRISMOND DAVIES-SCOURFIELD

The Battle of Calais in 1940 has never attracted the attention which perhaps it deserves. This is hardly surprising: it took place when other more dramatic events were unfolding – the catastrophic defeat and occupation of France and the British Expeditionary Force's evacuation at Dunkirk. Calais, on the other hand, was fought on a comparatively small scale, just one panzer division against one mechanized brigade. Nevertheless there are features of the battle which justify considerable interest and study when brought out into the open.

For the British troops involved the battle has been described as 'a forlorn hope in an unaccustomed role.' It was a forlorn hope in that one British brigade, including one tank battalion, without artillery, engineer or air support, was pitted against a complete German panzer division backed by the resources of a whole panzer corps and the support of the German air force. It was an unaccustomed role in that the three British infantry battalions were all fully mechanized and specially trained, organized and equipped for mobile operations. Nevertheless, as a very young platoon commander, my lasting impressions of the battle are mainly of the professional acceptance by my riflemen of what was fairly obviously a hopeless situation, we being outnumbered, outgunned and trapped against the sea. They recognized and accepted that they had been sent to do a job and they were quietly determined that they were going to do it, to the best of their ability, right up to the end. No one questioned the job itself or the orders received, and no one ever asked me whether we were going to be evacuated and if not why not. It was professionalism at its best, laced with plenty of cockney humour. Arthur Bryant was only too right when he once said that the natural home of the British Army was 'The Last Ditch, where it always excelled itself.'

This book, attractively written and carefully researched, provides a need which has long existed. It also provides a wealth of valuable information on how best to visit the battlefield,the places where the major actions took place together with the best viewing points, and with additional information on hotels, restaurants and car parks. Yet all this wealth of detail does in no way obscure Jon Cooksey's clear explanation on how and why the battle was fought and his very balanced view on what the importance of the battle may or may not have been, so that the reader can, without too much difficulty, draw his or her own conclusion.

6

Area covered in this guide

Map section from the original issued to Lieutenant Colonel Keller, CO 3RTR prior to his departure for Calais 22 May 1940.

INTRODUCTION

Calais. For many Britons today the name probably conjures up images of a swift journey beneath the English Channel aboard *Le Shuttle* bound for the vast rail terminal to the south-west of the town. For a good many more, however, Calais is synonymous with hulking cross-channel ferries and a huge, soulless ferry terminal constructed with the express intention of getting as many people on and off the waiting craft in the shortest possible time. In many respects such images are the only ones that many people who journey to the continent by car via this pre-eminent French ferry port will retain as they are guided in snake-like convoys from the bowels of the trains or, in the case of the ships, across acres of tarmac, over bridges and through underpasses to the Douane posts and on to the roads beyond.

Sightseeing at this point in the journey is most definitely out of the question unless one wishes to incur the wrath of the drivers of scores of vehicles crawling along behind, eager to get on to the motorway system which now runs right up to the terminals, and hare off to other parts of the continent or to the numerous hypermarkets or cavernous shopping malls which have sprung up to the south and west of the town. And here is perhaps another, more contemporary image of Calais. It is the image of the short-break, day-trip destination for tens of thousands of British 'trippers' who cross the channel each year, all year round, whether by ship or tunnel, seeking to stock up on cut-price crates of beer, wine, spirits and cigarettes.

Faced with stiff competition in the form of the fast crossing offered by the channel tunnel shuttle train service, *Le Shuttle*, the ferry operators had to decide on strategies to attract otherwise errant customers. This has led to collaborations with daily and Sunday newspapers in developing the culture of crossing the channel 'for a tenner', 'for a pound' or even 'for free', sometimes with a crate of beer thrown in for good measure. For those members of the public within reasonable striking distance of Dover a day trip to Calais is now as realizable and as affordable as a trip to Brighton or Clacton once used to be with the added bonus that a trip to Calais is a trip 'abroad'. Indeed, in the first two months of 1999 the Port of Calais handled more than 1, 750,000 passengers and almost 700,000 vehicles of all types of which 310,619 were driven by tourists.

These statistics and the relentless development in the immediate vicinities of the ferry and rail terminals bear witness to the increasing popularity of Calais as the major port of entry to France. For many, like myself, the distant view of Calais as a smudge on the horizon above the starboard bow of a cross-channel ferry was our first view of France, of another country, of 'abroad'. For me as a youngster, Calais was the magical gateway to a culture and a way of life far removed from my own Northern upbringing. From the moment of that first sighting Calais has held a certain fascination for me as it represented new experiences and an adventure into the unknown.

I and millions of other Britons were following in the wake of some of British history's most illustrious figures as we sailed out into the Straits of Dover on the short crossing to France. For centuries Calais, due to that mercifully short crossing and its relatively good access to Paris, has been a favoured port of entry for Britons crossing to and trading with France. Such a location inevitably meant that Calais would become the focus of military struggles as the avaricious leaders of various nations fought for possession of the port and the prize of economic and military advantage.

Siege and encirclement have thus often played a part in its turbulent history. It was beseiged by Edward III in 1346 after his victory over the French at Crecy and was finally captured after a dour defence in 1347. In a now famous postscript to the siege, six Burghers of Calais were handed to Edward in return for sparing the lives of the rest of the townspeople. They were saved after Edward's Queen, Philippa of Hainault, interceded on their behalf. The Burghers now stand ,chained as they were six hundred and fifty two years ago, immortalised in bronze by the sculptor Rodin, in front of the Hotel de Ville.

Another English monarch, King Henry VIII, would have sailed from England into the harbour and used Calais as a base for part of the time during his negotiations with Francis I and Charles V in the early 1500's. The town was attacked again in 1558, this time by the French who succeeded in wresting it from English control. The loss of Calais and all that it meant to her so moved Mary Tudor that she was reported to have said, 'When I am dead and opened, you shall find "Calais" lying in my heart.' She died in the same year that Calais fell to the French. Less than ten years later it was attacked again and changed hands again, this time falling to a Spanish force under King Philip II. Fortified by Vauban, the French military architect, in the seventeenth century and set amongst a labyrinth of ditches and canals, Calais became a formidable obstacle to any force wishing to gain control of this stretch of the north French coast. The British Army had a large base at Calais during World War One and many of Britain's sons would have steamed into its harbour and passed through its streets on their way to who knows what. The history of Calais is therefore rich in trial and tribulation.

With regards to the subject of this guide, the defence of Calais by 30 Brigade in May 1940, there are precious few contemporary accounts which could act as a guide for those with sufficient interest in the battle to follow with ease the actions on the ground.

The interested visitor often encounters problems in finding adequate material from which to plan a visit. Official unit records are sketchy in many cases and non-existent in others due to the nature of the fighting and the fact that very few of the combatants managed to make it back home alive across the Channel. Those who were not killed in action were taken prisoner and, with a few notable exceptions, were to remain in German captivity for the duration of the war. All that exists, for example, in the War Diary of the 2nd Battalion Kings Royal Rifle Corps (2KRRC) for that period is a typed letter of six lines' length written by the new Commanding Officer on 17 March 1942, to the Under Secretary of State at the War Office, stating that the battalion, 'proceeded to Calais on 22nd May, 1940, and suffered almost 100% casualties. This Battalion was reconstituted on 14th June, 1940, and no records of the old 2nd Bn. The King's Royal Rifle Corps are held.' PRO WO 167/60. There is no record of any war diary ever having existed for the other two battalions of infantry sent to Calais with 2KRRC.

A number of regimental accounts were published at a later date in an attempt to pull together the many fragments of what was a chaotic and bloody struggle consisting of countless isolated and personal 'battles', into some form of a coherent whole. Some of the participants lived with their memories for several decades before deciding to commit them to print and the scrutiny of publication. These accounts, like that of Brigadier Grismond Davies-Scourfield, are detailed, eloquent and moving, and are a vital addition to the literary canon of World War Two. Historians have good cause to thank these people for their wisdom in choosing to make their accounts public.

For many more involved in the Battle of Calais, however, their voices, for whatever reason, have not been heard. They are the memories of those survivors of the British Army who, dispatched so hastily by the British government amid a flurry of contradictory orders in an attempt to check the all-conquering German armour for as long as they were able, were handicapped by a lack of vital equipment and essential supplies. They are the memories of proud and resourceful professional and volunteer soldiers who believed in their abilities born of their upbringing and training, who believed in discipline and respect for their superior officers, who believed in their country.

For some of these their sense of bitterness stems from the way in which they feel that their beliefs and ideals were squandered by their political masters without any tangible gain. It is one of the aims of this guide to allow these people to tell their story and to add their perspective to the whole, since the events at Calais in May 1940 were, quite literally in some cases, life changing experiences.

Writing in January, 1999 from Western Australia where he has lived for the past forty years, Doug Wheeler, a veteran of the 1st Battalion The Rifle Brigade (1RB), wrote, 'I am 78+ years old, unable to remember much even from yesterday but can still recall CALAIS. It is carved on my heart like that old Queen.' Doug Wheeler was nineteeeen years old in 1940; soldiering and the Rifle Brigade were his life. His first view of France as a youngster would have been, like mine, the harbour of Calais, but his life path was not to lead him through a magical gateway to a rich and vibrant culture, it was to lead to war, to chaos and bloodshed and a further five years in prisoner of war camps. His war lasted just three days. All his training, his professionalism and his dedication to duty could not prevent his capture, the deaths of some of his closest friends and the destruction of his beloved regiment. 'It took me another eleven years' active service in two more wars 1947-1958 to regain my self-respect,' he wrote, 'We were the Best'.

It is my intention that the reader, through the pages of this book, be guided wherever possible by the voices of those who were actually there and to be transported back to a time when the fighting raged from barricade to barricade and from house to house; to a time of taut nerves, of fatigue, of heat, dust and raging thirst at the bridges, crossroads, in the cellars and on the narrow streets of this ancient French port. If those voices succeed in making some of the thousands of cross-channel passengers think of Calais as more than just a ferry port and a place to stock up the wine cellar for Christmas then the time spent in its production will have been worthwhile.

JON COOKSEY
Reading 2000

The Townsend Car Ferry Terminal in 1938, with the ferry _Forde_ berthed alongside the Quai de la Colonne Louis XVIII. Note the grassy slopes of Bastion 1 across the harbour and the tunnel which passed beneath it.

ACKNOWLEDGMENTS

A guide such as this requires the help, support, advice and guidance of a great many people. First and foremost I owe a great debt of gratitude to the surviving veterans of the battle of Calais who all gave freely of their time to talk to me about their experiences or to loan precious photographs, memoirs, maps or other illustrations for inclusion in the book. Many of the veterans agreed to read draft sections of the text and provided me with invaluable feedback. Of those who served with British units and fought in Calais I received encouragement and help from Mr Eric Chambers, Brigadier Grismond Davies-Scourfield, Mr Thomas Sandford, Mr Ron Savage (2KRRC), Mr Ray Archer, Mr Charles Green, Mr Doug Wheeler (1RB), Mr John Dexter, Mr T. Hammond, Mr Edward Lyme, Mr Jim Roberts (1QVR) Major Bill Close, Mr Jim Cornwell, Brigadier Hugo Ironside, Lieutenant-Colonel Bill Reeves (3RTR) and Mr William Harding (6 HAA Battery RA). I am grateful for permission to quote from the memoirs of Brigadier Davies-Scourfield, Mr Edward Lyme, Mr John Dexter, Major Bill Close and Lieutenant-Colonel Bill Reeves.

I am also grateful to Miss Yvonne Nulty, Mr David Davies and M. Henri Hidoine who have also given freely of their time to talk to me or loaned documents or photographs about life in Calais and their experiences as the Germans advanced through northern France towards their town between 10th and 23rd May 1940. M. Georges Fauquet, who also lived in the Old Town of Calais in May 1940, gave up a good deal of his own time to accompany me on a tour of some of the significant sites of the battlefield. I met Claude and Michel Delplanque whilst researching the tank action at Hames Boucres near Guines and I thank them for their help during that time, Whilst M. and Mme. Dupuy allowed me to visit 'Oyez Farm'.

I received a great deal of help from the families of men involved in the battle. Mrs Margaret Bishop and her son Mr Fred Bishop were kind enough to talk with me about Mrs Bishop's brother, Riflemen Don Gurr and Mrs Rosamund Kydd gave permission to use extracts from her late husband Sam Kydd's autobiography. I am grateful to Mr Richard Nicholson for permission to photograph and reproduce an illustration from the painting Last Stand at Calais by Charles Gere.

From institutions I have received considerable assistance from Mr Norman 'Tommy' Hummerstone, Secretary of the Queen Victoria's Rifles Regimental Association, Major Ken Gray of the Royal Green Jackets Museum and Colonel Ian McCausland, President of the King's Royal Rifle Corps Association. I owe a particular debt of gratitude to Major R D Cassidy who allowed me access to many documents during his tenure as curator of the Royal Green Jackets Museum and to Mr Richard Frost, Secretary of the King's Royal Rifle Corps, for his continued support and encouragement. Mrs Nancy Langmaid of the Tank Museum provided invaluable help and constructive criticism of the account of the action of 3 Royal Tank Regiment whilst Mrs J Harvey of the Regimental Headquarters of the Royal Tank Regiment was unfailingly courteous in responding to my many requests for help.

The staffs of the Public Record Office and the Liddell-Hart Centre for Military Archives at King's College, London have also provided help and assistance during my research as have the staff of the reading room at the Imperial War Museum. At the Commonwealth War Graves Commission Mr Derek Butler, Mr Peter Stainthorpe and Mrs Jacqueline Withers responded promptly to my many communications as did Frau Martina Caspers of the Bundesarchiv in Koblenz, Germany. In France, M. Jean-Pierre Vilbonnet of the Institut Geographique National, Madame Daussy of the Calais Economic and Tourist Development Office and Nicolas Marliot, Secretary of the Second World War Museum, 'Message Verlaine' in Tourcoing, have provided invaluable assistance. I thank them all for their efficiency, time and patience.

Several friends have volunteered their services during the writing of the guide and I extend my sincere thanks to Ghislaine Pearce and Josephine Jukes whilst Dick Hayes also provided much useful information. I owe a special debt of gratitude to Herr Hugo Stockter in Germany who has undertaken much research on my behalf and has translated a tremendous amount of material. His thoroughness and knowledge have helped to provide a German perspective to the battle for Calais which would otherwise have been lacking. Extracts from the papers of Rifleman Thomas Sandford held by the Imperial War Museum are reproduced by permission of the Trustees and Mr Thomas Sandford, whilst those taken from documents held by the Liddell-Hart Centre for Military Archives are reproduced by permission of the Trustees of that institution.

Ten years ago I was fortunate enough to be invited onto the research team, formed by Sir Nicholas Hewitt, to work on a formula for a series of guides to the battlefields of Europe. Since then I have observed the series growing from strength to strength, allowing many talented historians to share their knowledge and expertise with a wider audience. I make special mention of the support and advice of the team at Pen & Sword, and particularly Roni and Paul Wilkinson who have been responsible for the design work. It has been a pleasure to work with the team again.

Although a great many people have contributed to the guide it should be pointed out that any errors or omissions which still reside in the text are due entirely to me.

Finally, I am indebted to my wife Heather, who has been my greatest source of encouragement and my sternest critic. For her enduring patience and that of my daughter Georgia, I am truly grateful.

CALAIS TODAY

Looking at a modern map of the town of Calais may bring the shape of a human heart to mind. On the map Calais lies tilted slightly to the left; its shape defined to the west by the Canal de la Rivière Neuve and the railway, to the south by the A16 motorway and to the east by the line of the near straight watercourse which starts near le Virval, and runs north almost as far as the ferry terminal. These lines still shadow the outline of the nineteenth century earthworks and fortifications which formed the outer perimeter in 1940.

What look like the right and left lower chambers are divided by the Canal de Calais, separating Calais St. Pierre from the modern suburb of Nouvelle France much as it did in 1940. The two upper chambers of the heart shape are separated from those below, first by the Boulevard Leon Gambetta which drives straight into the heart of town from Coquelles in the west as it always has and by the Canal de Marck which does the same from the east. Further north are the valves; the bridges which cross the canals surrounding the Old Town providing the vital link with the southern suburbs as they have done since the union of the two towns old and new. There may have been a name change here and some construction work there - the centre of the three bridges is now called Pont Georges V and not Pont Richelieu for example, and the course of the road from Pont Freycinet past the Citadel has been altered and straightened – but the bridges are in the same place. Beyond Calais Nord to the north lies the main artery of the harbour, the major factor in the early growth and continued importance of the town. Further still are the breakwaters pointing out into the English Channel towards trade and links with Britain. On the map the shape of the town, due to the endurance of those strong physical features, does not appear to have changed a great deal in the last sixty years but the lines and contours on a map cannot show the tremendous pace and scope of development that has taken place during the last six decades.

The Calais of today does not obviously present itself as a battlefield, like many of those of the First World War. There are no remains of trenches or shell holes here for the visitor to stand in or trace from chalk slicks on the ground as there are on the rolling uplands of the Somme. There are no mine craters to stand in and wonder at, no vast cemeteries which catch the breath like the one at Tyne Cot in the Ypres Salient. Calais is a busy working port and industrial town with an agricultural hinterland and as such it is responding to the ever-changing needs of internal and external markets. Much has changed, even during the last ten years, not least in terms of the infrastructure of the town and its surroundings. The siting of the Channel Tunnel terminal near Coquelles, just beyond the town's limits to the south-west, and the ever-increasing volume of cross-channel ferry traffic have been the prime factors in the extensive development of the motorway and rail networks in this part of the region of the Pas de Calais. In addition to building new roads, railways and terminals other construction work has seen a rash of new industrial and commercial zones spring up to the west, south and east, of which the vast Cité Europe site near the tunnel terminal is just one example. There are well over a thousand hotel rooms in and around Calais today and scores of brasseries and restaurants. There are new housing developments, an established university, large modern colleges and a large, state of the art sports complex as befits a town entering the 21st century.

For the visitor interested in the battles of 1940, however, much of the construction work of the last decade has also swept away most of what remained of the physical evidence of the fighting at key sites even though a glance at a modern map may suggest otherwise. Ten years ago it was still possible to see a much truncated grassy mound which was the remnant of Bastion 1 near the inner harbour, as well as the distinctive shape of the white water tower near the Gare Maritime, a well-known landmark for many soldiers during the final stages of the battle. More importantly the memorial to the Green Jackets, unveiled on 2 June 1951, in the presence of Field-Marshal Montgomery in memory of those riflemen who fell defending Calais, still stood on the site of their final stand. There is precious little to see now, however, in the immediate vicinity of the ferry terminal which was the scene of bitter fighting on Sunday 26 May 1940, as the men of 1 Battalion The Rifle Brigade (1RB) and elements of 2 Battalion The King's Royal Rifle Corps (2 KRRC) and 1 Battalion The Queen Victoria's Rifles (1QVR) made their final stand. The grassy mound and the water tower are gone. So is the Green Jackets' Memorial. The construction work which has gone on in pursuit of greater efficiency in handling increasing numbers of ferry passengers has been at the expense of many tangible reminders of the struggles which took place in that particular area on the last day of the battle. There is still a good deal to see beyond the ferry terminal, however, if the imagination is allowed a little freedom. Thankfully the Green Jackets' Memorial did not disappear for ever. In 1996 agitated Calais veterans began to contact Regimental Headquarters in Winchester with reports that the memorial had disappeared. The Calais Harbour Authorities, anxious to press on with redeveloping the ferry terminal, had dismantled it and stored it in containers without seeking permission. After some discussion a new site, both accessible and visible, was chosen on the Western entrance to the inner harbour, just north of the municipal camp site which now stands on the site of Bastion 12. The Port Authority agreed to pay for the re-erection of the memorial and the Royal Green Jacket Administrative Trust pledged £8,000 for the making of a new cross in consultation with the Commonwealth War Graves Commission. The memorial was re-dedicated at a special service on Wednesday, 20 May 1998, at which forty-seven Calais veterans paraded under the command of Brigadier Grismond Davies-Scourfield whom, as a Second Lieutenant, had been wounded three times and captured at Calais.

Apart from the Green Jackets' Memorial it is still possible to visit various points in and beyond the town and reflect on what it must have been like for those involved in the siege, for the battle of Calais was in many ways a set-piece action where the Allied troops made use of pre-existing defensive positions. In this respect alone one can draw parallels with set-piece actions of World War One. This is particularly true of sites such as Fort Nieulay, now being sympathetically restored by the Town Council with financial assistance from the central government, the Citadel and Fort Risban in Calais Nord. Although Calais Nord was practically razed to the ground by German bombers and artillery in 1940, a situation made worse by the Allied bombing prior to the town's liberation in 1944, it is still possible to find and explore certain features and fortifications which held particular significance for the British and French defenders and their German assailants.

The re-dedication of the Green Jackets' Memorial on the western jetty at Calais, 20 May 1998.

A Note on Using the Guide and Advice for Visitors

It is essential to understand the 'now' in the context of a guidebook if one thinks of the tremendous pace of change in Calais during recent years! It is all too easy to neglect unknowingly the site of some action due to the accumulated developments of more than half a century.

Talking of steps, Lord Macaulay once wrote that , 'knowledge advances by steps and not by leaps,' and in terms of a guide book I could not agree more. Personally I have always found it is essential to get out on to the ground and follow in the footsteps or tracks of those who made history here, hoping with each step I take, to increase my knowledge of what happened and why, to make connections and to try to understand. In the Old Town there is no need to do anything other than walk. With a battlefield such as Calais, however, with quite long distances involved in visiting sites beyond the outer perimeter – the initial positions of 1 QVR involved a deployment along a front of some thirty kilometres for example – it is essential to have some form of transport to get from one site to another. Experienced cyclists should not find the distances involved too taxing, but for most of us the means of transport will be a private car or mini-bus.

In preparing this guide I have assumed that many readers will want to get onto the ground and walk and a number of suggested routes can be found towards the end of the book. I am also aware, however, that for a variety of reasons there may be some readers who will find some of the walks difficult to negotiate and with this in mind one of the routes has a 'short' and 'long' version. In addition a number of tours by car are suggested.

For those who wish to walk I can do no better than reiterate the excellent advice to be found in other guide books in the *Battleground Europe* series. In the town itself you are never very far from a drink or bite to eat at any one of the many bars and restaurants. Some of the tours may take several hours to complete and pounding pavements, whatever the weather, can be exhausting so strong shoes or a pair of the lighter, 'urban' walking boots are a good idea. In the summer it is a good idea to carry sun cream, a hat and something to drink.

Some of the tours take the visitor out into the countryside along footpaths and tracks and through small villages where there is little by way of food and drink so it is advisable to pack enough food and drink to last several hours. Again in summer it is wise to take precautions to avoid excessive exposure to the sun. Hay fever sufferers amongst us should be well prepared with medication. It is advisable to pack a first aid kit, complete with sting relief. In winter, waterproof walking boots or Wellingtons are ideal for tramping through mud or wet grass and a spare set of socks may come in handy.

A good quality map case which hangs around the neck leaving hands free to use a compass or a camera or to jot notes down in a notebook is a very practical addition to the equipment list. It will ensure that your papers are kept clean and dry for the most part. (See A Note on Maps below) I have always found that a small pencil case with a selection of pens, pencils and highlighters useful to mark up interesting locations or your own variations to routes. A dictaphone is also a boon to enthusiasts who may wish to record their visit in more detail than they would normally be able to do with pen and paper. In that case spare tapes are a must as are spare films for the camera. A medium-sized rucksack or 'daysack' will enable you to carry everything on your back comfortably.

A Note on Maps

As well as the maps to be found in the guide, professionally prepared present day maps of the area are essential items. One can never have too many maps but at the very least one should carry the French Institut Geographique National (IGN) map depicting the whole of the area, plus a street map of the town. The list below identifies those which I have found most useful:

1) IGN Serie Bleue (Blue Series) entitled *Calais: Site des Caps, Forêt De Guines* (2103 ET) 'Top 25'. Scale 1:25 000 (1cm = 250 m). The IGN performs almost the same function as our Ordnance Survey. This map covers the whole of the designated area in great detail and includes contours and other topographical features. If you were only to buy one map then this would be it. Fortunately the map is also one of IGN's *Top 25* series which covers the coastline, forests and mountain regions of France and includes a wealth of additional tourist information which does not appear on most other Blue Series maps.

2) IGN Thematic France Series entitled *Forts & Citadelles, Musées Militaires* (907). Scale 1:1000 000 (1cm = 10km). Covers the military architecture of the whole of France from Vauban to Maginot and shows the location of all the major fortifications and military museums with some interesting information on the reverse.

A free IGN catalogue is available from their British distributor, World Leisure Marketing and Map World (tel: 01332 343 332 fax: 01332 340 464) or from Hereford Map Centre (tel: 01432 266322 fax: 01432 341874, e-mail: mapped@globalnet.co.uk.

The IGN has its own web site at http://www.ign.fr

3) Commonwealth War Graves Commission (CWGC) entitled *Calais Lille Bruxelles*. This is the Michelin Map (51), Scale 1:200 000 (1cm = 2km) overprinted with the locations of Commonwealth war cemeteries and memorials. A detailed alphabetical index is also provided. Available from

the CWGC (tel: 01628 634221 fax: 01628 771208) The CWGC has an excellent web site at http://www.cwgc.org (e-mail: cwgc@dial.pipex.com) with a page dedicated to its publications.

4) Plan Guide Blay Foldex entitled *Calais*. Scale 1: 9 500 (1cm = 95m) A useful street map, particularly good in assisting the study of the battlefield up to and including the line of the outer perimeter although it does not extend much beyond that boundary. Some useful addresses and telephone numbers are   printed on the reverse along with additional tourist information in English. Obtainable from the Calais Tourist Office, 12, Boulevard Clemenceau, 62100, Calais (tel: 321 96 62 40 fax: 321 96 01 92 e-mail: ot@ot-calais.fr) or from Blay Foldex 40-48 Rue des Meuniers, F-93108, Montreuil, Cedex, France. (tel: 149 88 92 10)

5) Editions Grafocarte, Plan Guide, Bleu & Or entitled *Calais*. Scale 1: 13 300 (1cm = 133m) Another clear map making good use of colour and this time extending some way beyond the line of the outer perimeter to include the villages of Coquelles – including the Eurotunnel terminal – Coulogne and part of Fréthun. There is a good deal of information on the reverse, including an alphabetical listing of street names and a separate map of Calais Nord to the scale of 1:12 000 (1cm = 120m) on the reverse. Editions Grafocarte 125, Rue Jean Jaques Rousseau, BP 40, 92132 Issy-Les Moulineaux, Cedex, France. (tel: 141 09 19 00 fax: 141 09 19 22)

It is also worth bearing in mind that many companies publish free maps of the town of Calais as a way of advertising local products or services. These can be picked up from the Calais Tourist Office and a number of shops. Many of these maps are restricted to showing the town up to or a little way beyond the outer perimeter but each one shows something a little different. Try to obtain the most recent editions of maps. The numbers and routes of some of the footpaths shown on the IGN sheet 2103 ET, for example, do not, in some cases, equate to the route on the ground and many of the maps, some of them obtained in 1998, still show the Green Jackets' Memorial as standing in its original position on the eastern side of the inner harbour!

Whether in town or country it is wise to observe certain common sense rules with regard to safety and the local inhabitants whilst we are visiting the battlefield. Park cars with care, particularly on roads and lanes in agricultural areas, and always lock valuables and bags that you do not need out of sight in the boot of the car. Observe any *propriété privée* and other warning notices and exercise care in and around some of the old fortifications by sticking to marked paths and safe areas as indicated. At Fort Lapin signs quite clearly tell the visitor of the dangers of falling masonry. Accidents can and do happen, so make sure your tetanus jabs are up to date. In addition to any personal accident insurance you may arrange privately it is always a good idea to carry form E111. This is issued free and is attached to a booklet, obtainable from larger post offices, explaining your entitlement to hospital and medical treatment in France and other European countries.

Calais is now more accessible than ever, with the ferry companies and the tunnel operators vying for our custom. It is possible to catch an early morning train or ferry and spend the best part of ten hours in Calais before making an evening crossing for the journey home. The various three and five day deals offered by the cross-channel operators are also ideal for visitors to Calais. The possible downside of improved accessibility is the risk of increased familiarity which could trip up the unwary. It is tempting perhaps, and especially so on a day visit, to forgo the usual travel precautions of comprehensive personal and vehicle insurance, but it is wise to ensure every member of the party and the vehicle is adequately covered. Some of the motoring organizations now offer free breakdown and legal expenses cover for up to seventy-two hours for the cost of a 'phone call. It should also be remembered that Third Party cover is a minimum requirement when travelling in France. Green cards are no longer required as evidence of minimum cover as inspection of these documents has been abolished at the frontiers. It is advisable, however, to tell your agent or broker of your intended travel plans to ensure that your cover is extended to apply. Failure to do so may result in the policy being restricted to the minimum requirements necessary for the insurance of vehicles in France. The list of 'compulsory' items to be carried by motorists as required by French law is also an essential, be it a day trip or a two-week stay. These include your licence and vehicle registration documents, a warning triangle, headlamp beam converters and the visible display of the GB plate. Children under the age of ten are not allowed to travel as front seat passengers in France. Carrying a spare set of bulbs, whilst not compulsory, is highly recommended.

Calais is also blessed with abundant services and a wealth of hotels and restaurants, split between the old and new towns, to suit every taste and pocket.

The following list of hotels, some with restaurants, may provide a useful starting point. It is possible to turn up at a hotel and find a comfortable room or to book one through the Tourist Office. To call for reservations from the UK dial 00 33 , followed by the nine digit number given. (If you come across a ten digit number dial the 00 33 code from the UK and knock off the first 0 of the French number.)

Hotels in Calais:

Metropol ***, 43, Quai du Rhin, 62100 Calais. Tel: 321 97 54 00 Fax: 321 96 69 70

e-mail: MetropolHotel@metropolhotel.com. Situated close to the southern end of Pont Freycinet and a short walk from the Citadel. Comfortable and well appointed rooms.

Hotel Georges V ***, 36 Rue Royale 62100 Calais. Tel: 321 97 68 00 Fax: 321 97 34 73

e-mail: GeorgeV@GeorgeV-calais.com One of the larger hotels on the main shopping street in the heart of Calais Nord. Chosen as the lunch venue for members of the KRRC,RB and QVR Club Members after the re-dedication of the Green Jackets' Memorial on 20 May 1998.

Hotel Richelieu **, Rue Richelieu 62100 Calais. Tel: 321 34 61 60, Fax: 321 85 89 28. Situated on the street opposite the Parc Richelieu a short walk from the Rue des Marechaux which was used as a line of defence by 2KRRC during the latter stages of the battle. It is a few doors away from the Musée des Beaux-Arts et de la Dentelle. A 'no nonsense' hotel with a little private parking to the rear but not really suitable for disabled people.

Hotels Beyond Calais:

Copthorne ***, Avenue Charles de Gaulle, 62231 Coquelles. Tel: 321 46 60 60, Fax: 321 85 76 76

e-mail:Copthorne@copthorne.com Built on the site of the Château Pigache position held by the Germans and taken by the Allies in September 1944, and opposite the wooden windmill on the Coquelles Ridge. It is on the route taken by some of the tanks of 3 Royal Tank Regiment (3RTR) on their way to meet elements of the German 1 Panzer Division near the village of Hames Boucres.

Hotel Normandy **, Place de Verdun, 62179 Wissant. Tel: 321 35 90 11, Fax: 321 82 19 08. Situated some fifteen minutes by car along the D940 coast road from Calais it is now run by Didier Davies, the latest member of the Davies family to run the hotel. Didier, trained as a chef in some of the top restaurants in France and is the son of David Davies who owns and runs the Atlantic Wall Museum housed in the German Battery Todt at Audinghen a little further along the coast. David's father, a Welshman who served with the Royal Welch Fusiliers in World War One, stayed in France and married a French girl and went on to run the Hotel. As a boy David had been one of the last civilians to leave Calais on 23 May 1940, due to his father's British citizenship. He is often in the hotel and has a wealth of knowledge about the history of the region and the German Atlantic Wall defences in particular. Most of the Normandy's 28 rooms offer sea views, and it boasts an excellent restaurant.

Camping:

This is a small selection in no particular order of merit. There are several other camp sites in the vicinity. Contact the Calais Tourist Office for more information. Again, do check on facilities and dates of closure or otherwise before departure as these can be subject to change at short notice.

Camping Municipal de Calais **, Avenue Raymond Poincare, 62100 Calais. Tel: 321 97 89 79/

321 34 73 25. Situated right on top of the site of Bastion 12 and next to Fort Risban overlooking the harbour, the site has 256 pitches which includes caravans and is open all year round.

Les Peupliers **, 394 Rue de Beaumarais, 62100, Calais. Tel: 321 34 03 56. This camp site lies outside the outer perimeter a little over one kilometre beyond the Porte de Dunkerque and very close to the Cimetière Sud which

The casemate which housed a 380mm gun, and which was aimed across the Channel, is now the home for the *Musée de Mur de l'Atlantique*.

is the last resting place of many of those killed in action at Calais. It has 56 pitches with spaces for caravans and is open all year round.

La Belle Peche *, Route de Guines, 62340, Hames Boucres. Tel: 321 35 21 07, Fax: 321 82 51 50. A camp site close to the heart of the battlefield fought over by the tanks of 3RTR and 1 Panzer Division on 23 May 1940. Closed 1 October until 1 April.

A Note About Calais on the Internet

Before we leave this section of the guide it is worth spending some time looking at Calais on the World Wide Web for those readers who are already using the Internet and for those who have yet to go 'online' but who nevertheless have access to the net via their local library or university. I would like to draw readers' attention to the highly professional web site developed by the Calais Tourist Office which can be found at http://www.ot-calais.fr

One page of the site will attract the attention of those interested in deepening their knowledge and understanding of military history and this is the '39-45 Route'. This route, promoted by the Calais Tourist Office, brings together eight museums or sites of significant interest related to World War Two, five of which are within easy striking distance of Calais. The web page does not go into detail about each one of the museums or sites, so details are listed below. As opening hours and admission charges are subject to change I would advise contacting the sites direct for up to

date information in order to save wasted journeys.

Musée de la Guerre, Calais, Parc St Pierre 62100 Calais, (Tel: 321 34 21 57) Situated in the middle of the Parc St Pierre, opposite the Hotel de Ville, the Calais War Museum is housed in 20 rooms of the 94 metre long 'Mako' bunker built by the Germans as a central telephone exchange and HQ of the Port Commandant during the occupation. Among the exhibits is a section devoted to the Green Jackets and the battle of 1940.

Musée de Mur de l'Atlantique – Batterie Todt, 62179 Audinghen, Cap Gris-Nez, (Tel: 321 32 97 33/ 321 82 62 01, Fax: 321 82 19 08) Owned and run by Mr. David Davies, the Museum of the Atlantic Wall is just off the D940 south of Audinghen. It is housed in one of seven bunkers built to protect a 380mm German naval gun and exhibits extend over ten rooms with vehicles and a 280mm K5 railway gun outside.

Historique de la Seconde Guerre Mondiale-Ambleteuse, 62164 Ambleteuse (Tel: 321 87 33 01, Fax: 321 87 35 01) twenty-five minutes from Calais along the D940 coast road or exit 7 from the A16 motorway (signposted Marquise, Rinxent) the World War Two Museum is on the left hand side of the road in Ambleteuse when driving in the direction of Boulogne. Laid out over 800 square metres the exhibits and displays follow a chronological order from the Polish campaign to the Hiroshima bomb. Special features include a street in Paris during the occupation and a video film about the Normandy invasion shown in a '1940's cinema'.

Mimoyeques, 62250 Landrethun-Le- Nord, (Tel:321 87 10 34, Fax: 321 83 33 10) Site of the famous 'Canons des Londres', the 'London Guns'. Five bunkers were built each housing five, 150mm guns 130m in length, with the aim of firing directly on London.

V2 Base – The Bunker of Eperleques, 62910 Eperleques, (Tel: 321 88 44 22, Fax: 321 88 44 84, web site at www. audomarois-online.com) This huge bunker in the forest of Eperleques was built as the first launch base for the German V2 rocket. Classified as a national historical monument in 1985, a laser CD takes the visitor through the history and technology of the site.

The three other sites which complete the '39-45 Route' are a little further afield. They are the **Musée de la Seconde Guerre Mondiale, 'Message Verlaine' – Tourcoing** near the Belgian border, **The Atlantic Wall Museum** in Ostend and the **Fort de Breendonk** north of Brussels. Not part of the '39-45 Route' but five kilometres from St Omer is **La Coupole**, the V2 bunker of Helfaut Wizerne 62504, St.Omer, (Tel: 321 93 07 07, Fax: 321 39 21 45). Uniformed hostesses act as guides for a tour lasting up to two hours which takes in the underground galleries, ascent into the five metre thick concrete dome which protected the V2 launch pad and films or audiovisual presentations in two cinemas each with 100 seats.

CHAPTER ONE

A TICKET TO THE TERMINUS

On 4 June 1940, Churchill stood in the House of Commons and delivered his, 'we shall fight on the beaches' speech in which he paid tribute to a 'British Brigadier' who had led a stubborn resistance in the face of overwhelming German forces. That 'Brigadier' was Claude Nicholson and his force, consisting of 1RB, 2KRRC, (60th Rifles) and 3RTR, – all regular troops from 1 Armoured Division, along with 1 QVR, a territorial motorcycle reconnaissance battalion of 1st London Division, had indeed fought in the streets and on the beaches of Calais. Many other personnel from Royal Artillery Searchlights units and other small parties joined Nicholson's Brigade during the fight. After four days the town was taken in the early evening of 26 May, and those who had survived the German onslaught were eventually taken prisoner but they had fought, in many instances, to the last bullet – a real fight to the finish.

In August 1948, Robert (later Lord) Boothby paid a visit to Winston Churchill who was holidaying at the Hotel Roy-Reine in Aix-en-Provence. At the time Churchill was revising his book The Second World War and had been working that morning on the advance of the German armour towards Dunkirk in May, 1940.

The German *Blitzkrieg* in the west, which exploded forward from positions on the Luxembourg frontier on 10 May is well documented. Responding to the codeword *Gelb* ('Yellow'), issued around midday on 9

PzKpfw 35(t)s rolling through a French field during the lightning thrust of the German armies towards the sea.

May the German forces had begun their astonishing advance across the frontiers of the Netherlands and Belgium towards the French border at 5.35 a.m. on 10 May. Plan Yellow decreed that the *Schwerpunkt*, the centre of gravity of the attack, would be concentrated in Army Group 'A' on the southern flank which had been allotted seven out of the ten Panzer divisions then in existence. These were part of the *Sichelschnitt*, the 'Scythe Stroke', a sweeping drive through the Low Countries and France which had the encirclement and complete annihilation of the Allied armies in the North as its objective At the southernmost tip of the scythe was General Heinz Guderian's XIX Panzer Korps.

At the age of fifty-two, Guderian was an audacious leader. He was the 'father' of Germany's Panzers, his theoretical work on the use of massed tank divisions, spurred on by other forward thinkers such as Britain's Captain Basil Liddell-Hart among others, led to his promotion to command Germany's first Armoured Corps in 1938. He was a master tactician in armoured warfare and had imbued his divisional commanders with his doctrine of co-ordinated assaults characterized by speed and mobility. They did not let him down.

'I had full confidence in my three divisional commanders; they knew my way of fighting and knew that when the Panzers started on a journey they had a ticket to the terminus. For us the objective was the sea. This was obvious!'

And that is just what they did. It took just ten days for the first of the Panzers to reach the sea. They had crossed the old World War One killing

Panzer crewman takes a breather from the cramped confines of his tank.

grounds in a matter of hours and by 7 pm on May 20 they had seized Abbeville. The sea was almost in sight. One tank battalion of 2 Panzer Division, the 'Spitta' Battalion, named after its commanding officer, was sent out and reached the mouth of the Somme at Noyelles as dusk closed in. The tank crews, who had crossed the Meuse scarcely a week earlier and had covered more than 250 miles in their cramped cockpits, jumped out and filled their lungs with the bracing air. They had reached the 'terminus'. They had cut a swathe through the Allied forces and had created an extended 'Panzer Corridor' which had cut vital road and rail communications between the Allied forces to the north and south of the corridor.

Guderian was eager to press on but his orders were slow in coming. By the time the German Army had issued its communique declaring, 'Our forces have reached the sea' on the morning of 21 May, Guderian was ready to go. Word had come through towards the end of the previous day that he was to turn north and he had begun to earmark his divisions for the tasks ahead of them. The 1st was to capture Calais, the 2nd was to invest Boulogne and the 10th was to advance towards the line of the Aa and push on to seize Dunkirk but events at Arras on 21st May were to alter Guderian's plans for an early resumption of the attack and ultimately delayed his assault on the channel ports. The Allied counter-attack at Arras with seventy-four tanks and the 6th and 8th Battalions of the Durham Light Infantry, supported by a force from a single French light armoured division, was not in itself a huge success, but it succeeded in striking a telling blow against the extended northern flank of the 'Panzer Corridor'. Guderian's advance had been so swift and decisive that a precarious gap had developed between the armoured and motorized units in the van of the assault and the supporting infantry following on foot, often two days march behind. To Hitler and the German command the largely British effort at Arras had been enough to convince them that their flanks were vulnerable and that Guderian should be made to apply his foot to the brakes, albeit temporarily.

As a result, General Schall's 10th Panzer Division was withdrawn from Guderian's

Heinz Guderian during the *Blitzkrieg* campaign in the west.

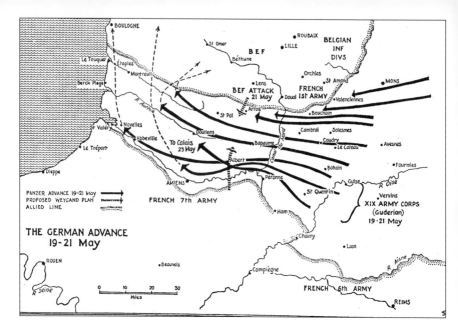

THE GERMAN ADVANCE
19-21 May

PANZER ADVANCE 19-21 May ➔
PROPOSED WEYGAND PLAN
ALLIED LINE

command at 6.00 a.m. on 22 May into Group reserve at Doullens. Shorn of a third of his force and feeling somewhat cheated in his grand design to take Dunkirk, Guderian decided to use his remaining two divisions in an advance up the coast to capture Boulogne and Calais. At mid-day permission was granted to allow the 2nd Panzers to drive up the N1 towards Montreuil and thence to Boulogne. The 1st Panzers were to move some five miles inland to provide protection for their eastern flank against attack from Calais. As the afternoon wore on and the 2nd Panzers came within site of Boulogne, Guderian received the welcome news that von Kleist had restored Schall's 10th Panzers to his command. Guderian,

British Army lorries leaving the Citadel at Calais via the Neptune Gate.

realizing that the prize of Dunkirk and the encirclement of Boulogne and Calais was again a possibility, decided to redirect the 1st Panzers eastward, to pass across the southern face of Calais and race on to cross the Aa Canal and thence to Dunkirk, whence the bulk of the Allied force in the north was retiring, a force which included the greater part of the BEF. If Dunkirk were to be taken then the Allied forces to the north of the Panzer Corridor would be beaten. The capture of Boulogne, and more particularly Calais, was not his priority. Guderian later expressed his view that there was 'no

28

particular urgency about taking this port.' If the Dunkirk domino fell and the Panzers succeeded in isolating any forces which could be landed at the two remaining channel ports, then sooner or later Calais and Boulogne would tumble.

With the 1st Panzers now directed to Dunkirk and the 2nd Panzers committed to the seizure of Boulogne where the 20th Guards Brigade had been landed by the destroyers *Vimiera* and *Whitshed* at 6.30 a.m., the job of taking Calais was handed to Major General Schall's 10th Panzers. His orders were simple and to the point, 'Capture Calais. Details of the enemy there not known'. Their task decided, General Schall began to draw up his plans for the taking of Calais and to make up for a little lost time. 'It seemed most important to the division,' wrote the divisional war diarist, 'to follow the rest of the XIXth German Army Corps and gain the Channel ports.'

Guderian's tanks of 2 and 10 Panzer Divisions rolled up the coast to Boulogne and Calais respectively to winkle out and mop up the defenders of those ancient ports. Boulogne finally fell on 25 May by which time 10 Panzer Division had been battering the force in Calais for the best part of two days. Being so close to home, no more than a two hour Channel crossing away, there was always the hope that Brigadier Nicholson's 30 Brigade would be evacuated just as the majority of 20 Guards Brigade had been from Boulogne a day earlier. Had not Nicholson received a message from the War Office in London to the effect that evacuation of his command had been decided 'in principle' during the early hours of 24 May? It was not to be. Despite the decision of the German High Command to halt Guderian's advance on Dunkirk on the same day, there would be no evacuation for the men of Nicholson's command. The deliberations of their own Prime Minister would see to that.

Just after 2pm on the afternoon of 25 May Lieutenant Austin Evitts of Number 12 Wireless Section, Royal Corps of Signals, walked over to the wireless truck parked in the inner courtyard of The Citadel. Lance Corporal Jordan was taking down a message.

'After he had finished it and made a final acknowledgement, he then handed it to me. It was from the Secretary of State for War, and as I read it I felt deeply moved, and proud, that to me and my wireless section had fallen the honour of transmitting and receiving so important a message. But there was more in his message than words could convey. It read as follows:

"1415 hours. To: Brigadier Nicholson Commander Calais
From: Secretary of State for War
Defence of Calais to utmost is of vital importance to our country and BEF and as showing our continued cooperation with France STOP The eyes of the whole Empire are upon the defence of Calais and we are confident you and your gallant regiments will perform

29

an exploit worthy of any in the annals of British history
Time out 1415 hours".'

The message was proof that Churchill was moving away from any thoughts of evacuation. Evitts was so moved that he made a copy of the message in his diary.

At 9pm that evening Churchill interrupted his dinner with the Secretary of State for War, Anthony Eden, and General Sir Edmund Ironside, Chief of the Imperial General Staff (CIGS) to draft the following message to Brigadier Nicholson:

> *'Every hour you continue to exist is of the greatest help to the BEF. Government has therefore decided that you must continue to fight. Have every admiration for your splendid stand. Evacuation will not (repeat not) take place, and craft required for above purpose are to return to Dover.'*

Hugo Ironside

So the defenders of Calais clung to their positions. Many hadn't eaten a decent meal or had a drink since they had arrived in the town. They were totally exhausted and supplies of ammunition were low. In Brigadier Nicholson's HQ in the Citadel a telephone rang in an empty cellar and was picked up by 2/Lieutenant Hugo Ironside, the young intelligence officer of 3RTR. On the other end of the line was his distant relative General Sir Edmund Ironside hoping to break the news personally regarding the decision not to evacuate. The two men exchanged a few words, the message was taken and 2/Lieutenant Ironside was told to carry on. Later a destroyer battled its way into Calais harbour to repeat Churchill's message but time was running out for the garrison. They fought on and continued 'to exist' until the following evening when they were finally overwhelmed.

In the warm, sun-filled room of the Hotel Roy-Reine three years after the end of the war, Churchill cast his mind back to those dark days of 1940 and told Boothby,

> *'I did Calais myself. I personally gave the order to stand and fight it out to the end. I agreed to the evacuation of Boulogne with reluctance; and I think now that I ought to have ordered them to fight it out there too. But the order to Calais meant certain death or capture for almost the entire garrison.'*

Tears began to fill his eyes as he continued,

> *'It was the only time during the war that I couldn't eat. I was very nearly sick at dinner. But together with the Gravelines line, which was steadily flooding, it gave us two vital days.'*

It was Churchill's view that the defence of Calais and the German decision to rest their armour on 24 May contributed directly to the salvation of the BEF on the beaches of Dunkirk.

CHAPTER TWO

BE YE MEN OF VALOUR

On 19 May, in his first broadcast to the British people since his installation as Prime Minister nine days earlier, Winston Churchill spoke of strong columns of German armoured vehicles 'ravaging the open country', penetrating deeply and spreading 'alarm and confusion in their track'. But he added, 'We must not allow ourselves to be intimidated by the presence of these armoured vehicles in unexpected places behind our lines.' The truth was that although Churchill had grasped the gravity of the big picture neither he nor Lord Gort at GHQ were aware of the finer details of Guderian's advance and exactly how many armoured vehicles constituted a 'strong column'. Information was often twenty-four hours out of date when it reached GHQ and even more when it reached London.

That the situation of the BEF was a cause for concern was not in doubt and it was clear that something had to be done to secure the Channel ports as a means of supplying the BEF and, if the worst came to the worst, getting them out. That same day discussions began under the code word

German infantry following up the panzers during the advance through France and Belgium.

A Luftwaffe 2cm flak team guard a river crossing point against an Allied air attack during Guderian's drive across northern France, May 1940.

'Dynamo' about the possible but 'unlikely evacuation' of a very large force under hazardous circumstances.

Churchill still believed that the situation could be stabilized by taking the fight to the Germans and breaking out southward towards the Somme and, in the light of the information he had to hand there was no reason to doubt that the Allies could not do so. He exhorted the British to 'Arm yourselves, and be ye men of valour, and be in readiness for the conflict'. And so plans to defend the Channel ports began to be made in an atmosphere of uncertainty, conjecture and out-of-date intelligence. The nature of the defence of Calais was to be coloured by the vague and nebulous nature of this early planning.

On the same day that Churchill made his broadcast the locals of Fordingbridge on the River Avon in the New Forest couldn't fail to notice that the road outside the Load of Hay public house was now deserted. Up until that time it had served as a rather conspicuous parking lot for twenty-seven, 14-ton cruiser tanks and twenty-one 6-ton Mark VI 'light' tanks, belonging to 3RTR. The tanks were in fact, on their way to Southampton to be hoisted into the holds of the cross-Channel steamer the *City of Christchurch*. The ship was bound for Cherbourg. Their crews did not go with them and it was the general opinion that the situation in France could not be so bad if they were not needed at once and that units going overseas would be able to train on French soil well away from the front line before being committed to battle. The lack of urgency was compounded by the fact that all the tanks had been loaded on to their transporters with a meticulous attention to regulations. Guns had been coated with a thick, sticky mineral jelly for protection and all sundry items had been broken down and packed in boxes to be itemized on regimental inventories. As the loading had got under way in earnest all petrol tanks had been drained and the petrol, all 7,000 gallons of it, stored in 4-gallon cans in wooden boxes stacked on deck. The *Christchurch* had been turned into a floating bomb!

This, it seemed, was not a regiment in a hurry to go into action. Filling a cruiser's petrol tank four gallons at a time was a lengthy operation. In addition, earlier that month a third of the battalion's complement had been transferred to form other units, the resulting gaps being filled by depot drafts. Surely these men would have to train for a good while yet before the full fighting efficiency of the regiment was realized once more. The newcomers hadn't even had time to sort out their kit in their new billets nor get to know much more than the names of their new crew mates before the battalion had been put on notice for a move to France where the 1st Armoured Division was assembling on the French tank training grounds at Pacy sur Eure between Rouen and Paris.

None of the men in these units, including the senior officers, knew it but soon they would be on their way to defend Calais. Their vague mission

30TH INFANTRY BRIGADE (The Green Jackets)

1 Bn The Rifle Brigade

Lt Col. Chandos Hoskyns

2 I/C Major A Allan

A COMPANY	B COMPANY	HQ COMPANY	C COMPANY	I COMPANY
Major J A L Taylor	Major A.G.L. Hamilton-Russell	Major H Coghill	Major V C Knollys	Major E J A H Brush
Captain P Peel	Captain M Smiley		Captain F A V Parker	Captain A Van der Weyer

2 Bn The Kings Royal Rifle Corps

Lt Col. E A B Miller

2 I/C Major O S Owen

A COMPANY	B COMPANY	HQ COMPANY	C COMPANY	D COMPANY
Major F L Trotter	Major J S Poole	Captain E R T Duncan	Captain M A Johnson	Major Lord Cromwell

1 Bn Queen Victoria's Rifles

Lt Col. J.A.M. Ellison-MacCartney

2 I/C Major T L Timpson

B COMPANY	C COMPANY	D COMPANY	HQ COMPANY
Captain G P Bowring	Major J Austin Brown	Lieutenant H V E Jessop	Captain J R G Palmer

3 rd Bn Royal Tank Regiment

Lt Col. R C Keller

2 I/C Major B C Mahoney

A SQUADRON	B SQUADRON	C SQUADRON	HQ SQUADRON
Major R H O Simpson	Major W R Reeves	Major F V Lyons	Captain Everett

1st Searchlight Regiment

Lt Col. R M Goldney

1ST BATTERY	2nd BATTERY

6th Heavy AA Battery, Royal Artillery

172nd Light AA Battery, Royal Artillery

229th AT Battery, Royal Artillery

would be to assist in escorting convoys to the BEF through a landscape where, it was thought, a few tired German tank crews supported by light machine-gun lorries and paratroopers roamed at will. It is just as well that neither they nor their political masters knew that there were at least seven hundred tanks from five Panzer divisions hunting in packs along the highways and by-ways of the Pas de Calais. Added to these was a brigade of mechanized infantry attached to each Panzer Division. In Guderian's XIX Korps a reasonable reduction of one third due to damage and battle casualties still put the figure of available tanks at more than 500 out of the 828 machines which had crossed the Luxembourg frontier on 10 May. Some 180 of these from 10th Panzer Division were destined to converge on Calais. A number of others from 1st Panzer Division would also play a significant part in the fighting south of the town. 3RTR had a little under fifty tanks on their way to Southampton to counter this formidable force. The odds were indeed daunting, and it was perhaps just as well that the British tank crews in Fordingbridge were blissfully unaware of them.

* * * *

In Calais itself the townspeople were no longer unaware of the ferocity of modern warfare. They had been in the middle of 'the conflict' for nine days by the time Churchill had broadcast his speech, suffering at the hands of the Luftwaffe. The bombers had come for the first time on 10 May and they had signalled to the Calaisiens a violent end to the *drôle de guerre*, or 'phoney war' which had existed since the declaration of war against Germany by Britain and France in early September, 1939.

Yvonne Nulty was a fifteen years old Calais schoolgirl, the daughter of a French mother and an English father who had never gone home after serving with the British Army in the First World War.

'On 10 May all hell broke loose. We began to be dive-bombed and as soon as the advance of the Germans was known all the defenders of Calais were moved up to the front towards Belgium and Calais became an 'open' town. That was a horrifying experience because there was nothing, but nothing to retaliate with. The dive-bombers would come and they would machine-gun the streets. I wanted to go out into the streets and watch. As a naïve fifteen year old it was very thrilling and exciting for me. I wasn't so much scared as wanting to see what was happening. You thought they were going to crash right into your house and then there was the terrible whistling of the bombs. I think they were trying to terrorize the population. They were attacking anything that was near the harbour and of course we were very close, living on the corner of the Rue du Thermes and the Rue du Madrid.'

Yvonne Nulty's days as a schoolgirl soon came to an abrupt end. The bombing of the town had become so fierce and unpredictable after 10 May

Fifteen years old Yvonne Nulty

that normal life had all but ceased to exist. She continued to make her way from her home in the Rue de Thermes and cross the bridge near the Place de Norvège to get to the High School for Girls behind the Hôtel de Ville for a few more days but it was becoming clear that her school career could not continue for much longer.

'Eventually the headmistress made us write a letter from her in our exercise books, informing our parents that in her opinion we should be kept at home until the fighting stopped. Those last few days at school were terrible. Every hour or so there was an alarm and all the classes would be taken to the crypt in the Hôtel de Ville. I spent my last few days at school having my lessons around the statue of the 'Burghers of Calais', in the crypt, where it had been put for safekeeping for the duration. I remember losing interest in the lessons because I kept looking at their faces and thinking what marvellous old men they were because they must have been in a war situation like we were.'

Now, as Guderian urged General Schall to draw up plans for the assault on Calais, the men of 30 Brigade enjoyed their last few hours on British soil. These were some of Churchill's 'men of valour' and they would need all the courage and resolve that they could muster in the days, months and years which, for some of them, lay ahead.

The Old Town, Calais 1940.

CHAPTER THREE

USELESS MOUTHS

Even as Churchill had made ready to speak to the nation on 19 May there were other British troops already in France whose valour would be tested to the limit in the battle for Calais. Lieutenant Airey Neave commanding 'F' Troop of the 2nd Battery, 1st Searchlight Regiment, Royal Artillery was one of them. He arrived in the village of Coulogne, south of Calais on 20 May after setting off from Arras the day before.

Neave set up his Headquarters in the Mairie opposite the church on the crossroads in the centre of the village and began to plan the role of his troop in the anti-aircraft defence of Calais. As he made his rounds that night, Neave took comfort from the fact that no bombs had, as yet, dropped on Coulogne and that, to him at least, there was little evidence of a breakthrough to the Channel ports. Thankfully for Neave the Luftwaffe did not venture further south that night and as he settled down to sleep in the Mairie he reflected that the Territorial Army had essentially prescribed a 'non-fighting' role for him and thoughts of being engaged in anything other than anti-aircraft defence never crossed his mind.

Airey Neave

(Survived the Battle for Calais and as a PoW escaped from Colditz. Served as Shadow Under-Secretary of State for Northern Ireland and was murdered by the IRA in 1979)

Anti-aircraft defence was also a high priority for Colonel Rupert T. Holland DSO, MC who, at the age of fifty-five, had been appointed Base Commandant of Calais at a conference called by the Adjutant General, Lieutenant General Brownrigg at the Imperial Hotel, Boulogne, at 6.00 pm On 19 May. Previous to Holland's appointment, Calais had served as an exit port for men on compassionate leave and had been served by just one boat service daily. His task, owing to the Germans now straddling the Allied lines of communication, would be to develop Calais as a Base Port for the BEF so that ammunition and supplies from England could be forwarded to formations in the field. He was also ordered to arrange for the evacuation of what were derogatorily referred to as 'useless mouths', essentially non-fighting personnel who would eat into precious food supplies if not returned home. There was also the question of evacuation of the wounded.

Old Calais before the storm that would destroy it.

If Calais was to operate successfully in its new role it would have to be defended from air attacks and changes would have to take place. Colonel Holland was to find that his job was by no means an easy one.

Early the next morning he drove to Calais and began to take stock of the situation.

> 'At 0800 hrs Major Douglas Hill and I left Boulogne for Calais by car... A platoon of Argyll and Sutherland Highlanders was guarding RAF special equipment on the eastern outskirts of Calais. Two transportation officers (Docks and Railways) arrived during the morning. Within the next 24 hours a Supply Officer... and a Transport Officer... reported to me. A Signal Centre already existed at the Civil Post and Telegraph Office in Boulevard Léon Gambetta. This became the Signal Office. A.A. units (guns and searchlights) had been detailed by the Major-General Anti-Aircraft Artillery, BEF for defence of Calais.'   PRO WO 217/2

In addition to the British forces there were French soldiers under the command of Chef de Bataillon Le Tellier in the Citadel, at Fort Risban and in position at several of the Bastions or guarding the main approaches into Calais. The coastal defences were under the command of Capitaine de Frégate Carlos de Lambertye with naval guns at Bastions 2, 11 and 12, the Bastion de l'Estran and at Fort Lapin. There was a machine gun section in Bastion 1

A rest camp was also organized on 21 May in the lace factory 'Duchene' 300 yards south of the Hôtel de Ville on the corner of the Rue de Pont Lottin

Stukas brought terror in to the hearts of the citizens of Calais.

and the Rue des Communes to house and feed the many men from numerous units who by now had begun to stream into town from all directions. Among these were some of the 'useless mouths' Colonel Holland had to repatriate. The anti-aircraft defences had begun to be strengthened on 19 May with the appointment of Lieutenant Colonel R. M. Goldney, Commanding Officer of 1 Searchlight Regiment since 1939, as

The docks at Calais under attack from the Luftwaffe who seemed to be able to bomb at will without interference from the Allies.

| **AVIS** aux | **AVIS** aux | **AVIS** à la |
| Militaires FRANÇAIS | Militaires Britanniques | POPULATIO |

(The posters read:)

AVIS aux Militaires FRANÇAIS

Les militaires français isolés doivent s'adresser tant pour le ravitaillement que pour le regroupement,

au CINEMA FAMILIA,
Place de la Nation

ou à la Caserne des Gardes Mobiles
près de la Citadelle

Calais, le 23 Mai 1940.

Le Maire
A. GERSCHEL

Vu le Commandant d'Armes
De LAMBERTYE.

AVIS aux Militaires Britanniques

Les militaires britanniques isolés doivent être dirigés tant pour le ravitaillement que pour le regroupement,

a l'Usine DUCHÊNE
rue du Pont-Lottin, (coin rue des Communes)

Calais, le 23 Mai 1940
Le Maire A. GERSCHEL
Vu le Commandant d'Armes
De LAMBERTYE.

NOTICE for the BRITISH SOLDIERS

The above british soldiers must be directed, as well for the nourishment as for the regroupement reassemblement towards

"USINE DUCHENE"
Pont-Lottin Street (corner Communes Street)

Calais, le 23 Mai 1940
The Mayor A. GERSCHEL
Vu le Commandant d'Armes
De LAMBERTYE.

AVIS à la POPULATIO

Par ordre de l'autorité militaire

Toute Circulatio
entre l'intérieur et l'extéri
de la Ville
est **INTERROMPU**

Des officiers et détachements français de la police de la Ville et interdiront tout stationnement sur la voie publique.

Calais, le 23 Mai 1940
Le Commandant d'Armes
de la Place de Calais
De LAMBERTYE.

NOTICE TO ALL FRENCH SOLDIERS	**NOTICE TO ALL BRITISH SOLDIERS**	**NOTICE TO THE POPULATION**
Isolated French soldiers must go to 'Cinema Familia' Place de la Nation, or to the barracks near the Citadel for food and ammunition and regrouping Calais 23 May 1940	Isolated British soldiers must be directed toward 'Duchene' Rue de Pont Lottin (corner of Rue des Communes) for food and ammunition as well as regrouping Calais 23 May 1940	By order of the military authorities. all traffic going in and out of town is interrupted. Officers and French detachments will act as police of the town and will forbid any parking on the public highway Calais 23 May 1940

Anti-Aircraft Commander Calais. His first HQ was at Ardres four miles south east of Calais.

His appointment and the convergence of men like Airey Neave on the Calais area were not before time. For as Lieutenant Austin Evitts witnessed as he sailed into Calais harbour with his wireless section at 6.45 pm on the evening of Tuesday 21 May, the Luftwaffe appeared to have a free hand to bomb Calais at will.

'Within minutes of our arrival the air raid warning sounded. Already we could see the bomb damage done in previous raids, several buildings around the docks had been destroyed, and some were still in flames. Then, almost immediately, enemy 'planes appeared in the sky right overhead. The

docks and harbour were again the targets for their attacks, and there appeared to be no ack-ack defence at all, nor did any Allied planes appear to intercept them, so they were able to do as they liked.'

Evitts' mission was to '...organize wireless communications for the BEF', if the worst came to the worst.Up to that time the navy had done the communications and now it was thought to be a job for the Army. Land lines in France and Belgium had been disrupted by bombing and if the only trans-Channel submarine cable link near Sangatte west of Calais was cut then it would be necessary to 'superimpose' the link by wireless. Evitts had been ordered to take three detachments and install wireless stations at Calais, Boulogne and Dunkirk, leaving a detachment in Dover Castle to act as control station.

After they had arrived and had weathered the bombing raid without damage to their equipment aboard the *Autocarrier*, they tried to make a start unloading, but the port of Calais was at a standstill. Evitts was told that it was impossible to unload as the derricks were unable to be used. German bombing had damaged the power station, the electricity was cut off and the civilian stevedores had gone to ground in fear of their lives. The skipper of the *Autocarrier* was extremely nervous and refused to wait all night at the quay side and risk destruction. He made it clear he was leaving but would return the next day. He also told Evitts that he had no extra food and that he and his men would have to go ashore. They were saved by none other than the Commanding Officer in Calais himself.

'Colonel Holland...who was in the Gare Maritime at the time came alongside and said accommodation could be provided for us that night at Garrison HQ...in the Boulevard Gambetta. Garrison HQ was in a building called La Clinique, a small very ordinary building, close to the road and which had probably been a nursing home of some sort. Here we had our first meal – bully beef and biscuits – and that night slept on blankets on the hard stone floor of the basement.'

There was a good deal of confusion during the next few days with apparently contradictory orders and a lack of control at the highest level. For a time it was not clear whether the Channel ports were to be defended at all.

Lieutenant Evitts left the Clinique early the next morning for the docks but was disappointed to find the *Autocarrier* nowhere in sight. He would have to wait another day for the arrival of his equipment. A few miles away that same morning, Colonel Goldney had driven from Ardres and set up his HQ at Orphanage Farm, set back from the main road half a mile east of Coulogne. In Coulogne itself Lieutenant Airey Neave was aware that rumours of a German advance in force in the direction of Guines were gathering momentum. He noted that increasing numbers of French civilians were converging on Coulogne from all points south in the hope of reaching the harbour in Calais and thus escaping the Panzers. During 22 May he received orders from Colonel Goldney that he should recall all his troop to HQ at the Mairie at dawn the next morning, and that he should busy himself with defending Coulogne as best he could by digging trenches to the south and south east of the village, and by building road blocks on all the roads leading into it. He would have seventy men with rifles, two Bren guns and a Boys anti-tank rifle which no one in Neave's troop had been trained to fire. As the trickle of frightened refugees turned into a steady stream throughout the day, the Searchlight personnel struggled to cope with their orders to prevent them approaching Calais. In spite of all this Neave still believed that the rumours of large numbers of German tanks were just that.

While Colonel Goldney was establishing his HQ at Orphanage Farm and Neave was busy preparing the defence of Coulogne, General Guderian's troops had also been on the move. Tired of sitting and twiddling his thumbs with two Panzer Divisions inactive for five hours on the line of the River Canche, he had characteristically jumped the gun by ordering his men forward forty minutes before the official command to advance. Within the space of two hours of the German push north from the Canche the first of the British troops from England who had been earmarked for Calais sailed into the harbour to help defend the town.

Churchill and Admiral Ramsay pore over charts at Dover Castle during the crisis brewing across the Channel.

CHAPTER FOUR

TANKS AND TERRIERS

In a twist of military fate some of the first troops to land were not regular soldiers but part-time Territorials of the 1 Battalion Queen Victoria's Rifles (1QVR), a formation which had helped to pioneer the volunteer movement and were descended from the Duke of Cumberland's sharpshooters of 1803. Rifleman Sam Kydd had been called up five days earlier to fulfill the obligations he had embarked upon the previous year and he had found his new 'family' to be essentially civilian in nature.

'The Queen Victoria Rifles were a mixed bag of Stock Exchange types and Cockneys from in and around Paddington and further afield...They were nearly all London blokes...very witty and sharp and good fun to be with...What the Cockney riflemen lacked in intellect they made up for with their natural wit, craft and friendly approach to everything...'D' Company, of which I was a member, were a pretty useful lot of all-rounders, which was shown when it came to games like football.'

Kydd was one of 566 officers and men under a new commanding officer Lieutenant Colonel JAM Ellison-MacCartney, the Bursar of Queen Mary College of the University of London who had served with the Territorial Army since 1924. 1QVR had wintered in

Sam Kydd
(starred in his own TV programme as Orlando during the 1960s).

Paddock Wood in Kent and later moved to Tonbridge where it had trained in its role as a Motor Cycle Reconnaissance Battalion (Divisional Cavalry) for 1 London Division. Its early training was done on borrowed civilian machines and in vans on extended loan. It had been mobilized in March 1940 for early service overseas and became part of 30 Infantry Brigade under the command of Brigadier Claude Nicholson when this was formed in April.

Although the 'Queen Vics' had received visits from Brigadier Nicholson himself, it had never trained with other units of 30 Brigade, namely the regulars of 1RB and 2 KRRC, and they were disappointed to learn on 11 May that they were to rejoin 1 London Division as Divisional Reserve in case of invasion. Eight days later Rifleman John Dexter and the rest of the battalion scouts drove through the night to hand over their twenty-two Scout Cars to 3RTR at Fordingbridge. Some of these were next seen standing driverless on the quay-side at Calais. So began a devastating litany of blunders which were to plague not only 1QVR, but other units of

Colonel Ellison-MacCartney

30 Brigade as they steeled themselves for active service. When the scouts returned to Ashford the next morning Colonel Ellison-MacCartney told them,

'"We shall be here for the next six weeks while our new Scout Cars are made." The very next evening TUESDAY 21 May, in great haste, we were put on the train at Ashford Station (with no vehicles – not even Wireless Cars or Dispatch Riders' Motorcycles) – embarked at Dover on the cross-channel ferry Canterbury *and landed in Calais the next day 22nd May, and behind us the 3rd Royal Tank Regiment arrived.'*

Colonel Ellison-MacCartney had been given no information as to his likely destination but even so the instructions he received were a nonsense for a battalion trained for a mobile role. Out of the 238 vehicles it had possessed in mid-May it was now being asked to go into action without so much as a staff car and with little if any training in conventional infantry tactics. The firepower of a motor cycle battalion was in any case much less than that of a regular motor battalion since a third of its number were drivers and therefore classed as cavalry. These men were issued with revolvers and some of those, like the one belonging to Rifleman Edward

Edward Lyme

Lyme had never been fired even in practice as , *'...there was no revolver ammunition; we were told not to draw it except to fire, but as it was empty anyway the instructions seemed superfluous.'* The officers were still unarmed when they eventually landed in France, they were not even issued with revolvers prior to departure.

The battalion left Ashford in two parties at 5.15 on the morning of 22 May, and arrived in Dover two hours later. The weather, mist and drizzling rain which greeted their early morning arrival, matched the mood of the men. Some of them heard the thud of gunfire carrying over the Channel from France. Up to that point no one knew where the battalion were bound and at Dover no one seemed to be any the wiser. The railway station was deserted. The sealed envelope which Lieutenant Colonel Ellison-MacCartney opened on the quayside was vague to say the least. His battalion, already without transport and vital communications equipment, was expected to land at Calais and take necessary steps to secure the town against 'a few German Tanks', which had, 'broken through towards the Channel Ports'. He was told that the remainder of 30 Brigade then in Suffolk, would follow next day and would land at either Calais or Dunkirk, but no one had told him that his battalion was once more part of that Brigade. As he began to digest these orders his men began to load their equipment onto the cross Channel ferry the *City of Canterbury* as the drizzle turned to pouring rain.

At almost the same time as Lieutenant Colonel Ellison-MacCartney was contemplating his written orders on the quay in Dover another commanding officer bound for Calais was grappling with a similar vague set of instructions.

Lieutenant Colonel Reginald Keller and the bulk of his battalion 3RTR, arrived in Dover at around the same time as 1QVR.

Keller was met by Major Foote, a Royal Tank Regiment officer seconded to SD7, the Royal Armoured Corps branch of the General Staff Duties Directorate at the War Office and was handed a bundle of maps and a sealed envelope like the one given to Ellison-MacCartney. Major Foote had been summoned the previous day by General Morris, the Director of Staff Duties in London and had been asked which unit of 1 Armoured Division was due to cross over to France that night. When Foote informed him that 3RTR was about to entrain at Fordingbridge for Southampton and that their tanks were in a ship at Southampton due to sail that night for Cherbourg. General Morris then told him that;

'... it had been decided to send a tank unit as quickly as possible to Calais to reinforce the Rifle Brigade in case Calais was threatened by the German advance. I was to motor down that night to Dover and tell Col. Keller of the change of plans. I realised that the unit would not have any maps of the area so I went round to the map depot and got a bundle of maps to give him at Dover. In the meantime two movements had been arranged for the trains and ship to be diverted and I set off by car to drive through the night to Dover. I met Col. Keller and 3RTR on Dover station platform about 5am. He was very angry and wanted to know what the hell was happening and where his tanks were. I explained the situation and gave him the last intelligence reports I had received before leaving London. I told him that his tanks would arrive in Calais that morning. He pointed out that all his tank guns were in mineral jelly and it would take at least a day to clean and zero them'. TANK MUSEUM

The envelope which Keller also received was addressed to the 'Senior

Military Commander, Calais'. To add to his irritation, however, Keller was not told the identity of this officer nor where he could be found. Keller's orders, like those of Ellison-MacCartney, were sketchy. In Keller's case a figure had been put on the number of German tanks threatening the Channel ports. He was told that seven light and four medium tanks were in the area of Boulogne and Calais. Colonel Keller could have been forgiven for thinking that this was some bizarre training exercise, had it not been for the urgency with which his regiment had been called into action. Less than twelve hours earlier he had been sitting in a Bournemouth hotel enjoying a pre-dinner drink with his wife when he had been called to the telephone. He was ordered to return at once to Fordingbridge and had left immediately by car.

Back in Fordingbridge many of Keller's men had been out on the town enjoying an evening drink when voices were heard in the street. They were the voices of MP's urging all 3RTR personnel to return to camp immediately. Notices had been flashed on the cinema screens of the Gaumont, the Royal and the Picture House in Salisbury interrupting the performances of the likes of Ginger Rogers and George Raft. By some colossal feat of organization the battalion had been on the train by midnight short of just one officer, Captain Barry O'Sullivan, and twenty men. They managed to catch up with the rest of the battalion an hour before they sailed for Calais.

They had no idea of their destination. All they knew was that their tanks had gone to Southampton and they assumed that they were going there too. By the early hours of 22 May they arrived in Dover. With no sign of their vehicle ship, the *City of Christchurch*, the battalion filed up the gangplanks of the *Maid of Orleans* along with a Dock Company of Royal Engineers and a few QVR. The remainder of a very damp QVR had by now finished manhandling their equipment onto the *City of Canterbury*, and the two ships steamed out of the harbour in a thick mist one behind the other at 11o'clock. They arrived in Calais at 1.15 pm.

Those first British troops to land were hampered by a frustrating mixture of adherence to military regulations and inept organization on the part of the higher authorities. This was compounded by a lack of logistical support and vital equipment. The scene which greeted Major Bill Reeves of 3RTR as the *Maid of Orleans* nosed into the quay was one of utter devastation.

Bill Reeves

Maid of Orleans, the cross-Channel ferry which took the men of 3 Royal Tank Regiment to Calais.

'I tried to reconcile the peacetime Calais with what it looked like now. The glass from the windows of the Customs House and restaurants was strewn all over the quayside and railway platforms. Black smoke was belching forth from most of the quayside buildings and warehouses and the whole area was pretty well pock-marked with bomb craters.'

Looking around them from the decks the men could see into the innards of houses broken apart by the bombs. Alongside the Quai de la Colonne the funnels and bridge of the tug boat *Calaisien* sunk during the first bombing raid on Calais on 10 May, were just visible above the water line and further into the harbour some of the lock gates joining the Avant Port with the inner basin had been smashed. Major T L Timpson, the QVR second-in-command, was met by an anxious embarkation transport officer who appeared somewhat bewildered and offered nothing in the way of useful advice. His only interest seemed to be in getting the *Canterbury* unloaded and turned round as quickly as possible in case of further air raids. The QVR began to unload their equipment manually as, on the previous day, there were no dock workers to be seen and there were no powered derricks in operation to make the job easier. Meanwhile, with no sign of the *City of Christchurch*, the troops of 3RTR began to disembark and move off to a safe area in the sand dunes east of the Gare Maritime. In the dunes, whilst some of the men smoked and chatted, others used their time to force bullets into the .5 inch machine gun belts manually in the absence of mechanical chargers causing much cursing and bruising of thumbs and fingers. Surveying the scene spread before him 2/Lieutenant Quentin

Carpendale's foremost thought was that it was 'a most extraordinary way to go to war.'

In the meantime Colonel Keller went in search of the addressee of his envelope. As soon as he stepped ashore he reported his arrival to a full Colonel but was brushed aside, the Colonel intent on leaving aboard the *Maid of Orleans* as soon as she could be turned around. Keller commandeered his staff car and drove off into town amid a mass of confusion as refugees rushed the gangplanks to try and make good their escape. It took him one and a half hours to find Colonel Holland in the Boulevard Léon Gambetta after being refused entry to the Hôtel de Ville on account of the fact that he had no official BEF identity card, yet another oversight due to his battalion's hasty dispatch. On his arrival at The 'Clinique' Keller handed the envelope to Colonel Holland who perused its contents and told him that his orders would come direct from GHQ at Hazebrouck. He then advised Keller to get his tanks off the vehicle ship as quickly as possible due to the close attentions of the Luftwaffe. Colonel Holland had already contacted London requesting air support and two Spitfires had arrived to chase off German bombers overhead. As a result the skies remained clear when loading eventually got under way later in the afternoon.

Colonel Ellison-MacCartney, who had issued orders to his company commanders for securing the harbour on landing whilst still on board the *City of Canterbury*, let his men get on with it and he also headed off to search for Colonel Holland to receive further instructions.

He returned to the harbour at 5 pm. having found Colonel Holland in the Boulevard Léon Gambetta and had been told that some light German armour had been sighted that very afternoon in the Forêt de Guines just a few miles south of Calais. Colonel Holland had not been informed of the arrival of 1QVR but he was glad to see fresh troops to bolster his meagre forces, and, although he appeared incredulous that a motor cycle battalion had been dispatched with none of its transport he nonetheless had a specific task in mind for the battalion. He ordered it to barricade the six main roads which converged on Calais from the west, the south and the east, whilst at the same time controlling the ever increasing wave of refugees which threatened to engulf the town and scupper military operations. They were also to secure the submarine cable terminal at Sangatte and patrol the beaches to east and west to prevent German aircraft landing at low tide. All these positions were beyond the outer perimeter. Ellison-MacCartney was to establish his HQ in Les Fontinettes.

'C' Company, under Austin Brown, were ordered to march east to block all roads leading to Dunkirk, Marck, Gravelines and Fort Vert and to patrol the eastern shore. Captain Bowring's 'B' Company was to defend the coast road west from Fort Risban near the harbour out towards Sangatte and patrol the beach for three miles. One unlucky platoon would have to go all the way to Sangatte itself, a distance of six and a half kilometres, to guard the submarine cable terminal. 'D' Company under Lieutenant Jessop were given the job of covering the roads leading into Calais from the south, from Fréthun, Guines and Ardres. It was a march of five kilometres south for the platoons of 'D' Company and although a few private cars had been commandeered at the docks by various companies the majority of the QVR had to carry everything.

The perimeter which Ellison-MacCartney was being ordered to defend was staggering for a force of some 550 men armed mainly with pistols and without any of its own transport. In effect they were being asked to secure a 'frontage' of some thirty kilometres, although they were concentrated at specific points along this 'front'. It was no easy task bearing in mind the great distances between companies and the difficulties of communication and co-ordination which these distances engendered.

The lack of transport now proved a serious handicap to all troop movement and communication and hampered adequate reconnaissance so that the hastily chosen sites for the initial roadblocks were not necessarily the most suitable for anti-tank defence. Under the circumstances the sites chosen were taken from the small-scale maps circulated to company commanders. As the companies finally began to move off to their allotted positions in the late afternoon it didn't take an expert to realize that their task in Calais would bear little resemblance to the one they had envisaged when they were finally sent into action.

'We ...were a motorized battalion and had been fully trained as a mechanized reconnaissance unit with scout cars and motor cycle and sidecar combinations upon which a machine gun was to be mounted to search out and account for the enemy – in theory that was – and in practice in England that was. But not in France. All of a sudden we were now Infantry and as Infantry we marched. This was for real. You can imagine the grumbling that went on. But nevertheless we marched.'

It was dusk by the time Sam Kydd arrived at his destination just beyond the ramparts to the south of Calais. Each of 'D' Company's three platoons was given responsibility for blocking one of the main roads into Calais. To the right of the company 'front' Sam Kydd and the rest of 11 Platoon under 2/Lieutenant R W Snowden were to block the road south west to Fréthun. A little over one kilometre south west of the line of fortifications and the outskirts of Les Fontinettes, 2/Lieutenant Snowden came to a hump-backed bridge over the Canal de la Rivière Neuve where the road ran parallel to the main railway line. He chose the dip on the near side of the bridge as the site of the block and his men went off to search for material with which to build it. The close proximity of the railway provided some ready-made obstacles.

> *'Our Company – 'D' – arrived at a pre-arranged position and then split up into platoons. Again we marched to another position – a minor road outside and leading into Calais – and there we awaited the arrival of the Germans. We mounted a road block in the form of some railway sleepers – the railway track was about two or three hundred yards away to our right- and we took up our positions, one section to the right, one to the left and another dug in behind a sandbag emplacement facing head on down the road.'*

In the centre, 12 Platoon under the command of 2/Lieutenant E B Brewester had orders to block the road to Guines. He halted his men some 700 metres south of the site of Bastion 8 at a point where the dead straight road which ran to the Pont de Coulogne intersected the Chemin de Grand Voyeu.

As 2/Lieutenant Glazier was marching his 13 platoon out along the Boulevard Victor Hugo to find a suitable site to block the road to Ardres and St Omer to the left of 'D' Company's front, a British Major told him to hurry as German tanks were reported to be advancing up the road about four or five kilometres away. 2/Lieutenant Glazier flagged down a passing truck and taking one section with him he set off down the road to St. Omer. At a point where the road forks to the right towards Guines he found the junction held by a French detachment, armed with an anti tank gun and two machine guns. When dusk fell and the rest of his platoon caught up, Glazier took up a position 500 metres beyond the Halte St. Pierre to the left of the French, covering a side road which led to a railway siding.

With everyone in position and with blocks hastily but finally prepared the men of 'D' Company were finally able to get some sort of rest in between bouts of sentry duty. On 11 Platoon's front Sam Kydd was woken from his fitful slumbers to take his turn on 'sentry go' for a two hour stretch from 2 am to 4 am on the morning of 23 May.

> *'At home I had never been very keen on guard duty but here it was worse. I hated it. It was eerie and scary – one spoke in whispers and a distant sneeze had you on the alert with the hairs on the back of your neck standing up in sympathy. Rifle at the ready with one up the spout you waited peering into the inky blackness.'*

Daybreak on the morning of 23 May saw the men of 1QVR scattered around Calais from the far flung outposts along the coast road to the west, at the barricades along the roads to Guines and Ardres to the south and out on the road to Marck and Gravelines in the east, and, like Sam Kydd, they were watching and waiting.

'B' Company were busy building a road block on the coast road towards Sangatte at Oyez farm with posts on the sand dunes and on the shore itself. 5 Platoon under 2/Lieutenant Dizer, the youngest officer on the strength, were ordered to move forward a further two and a half kilometres to

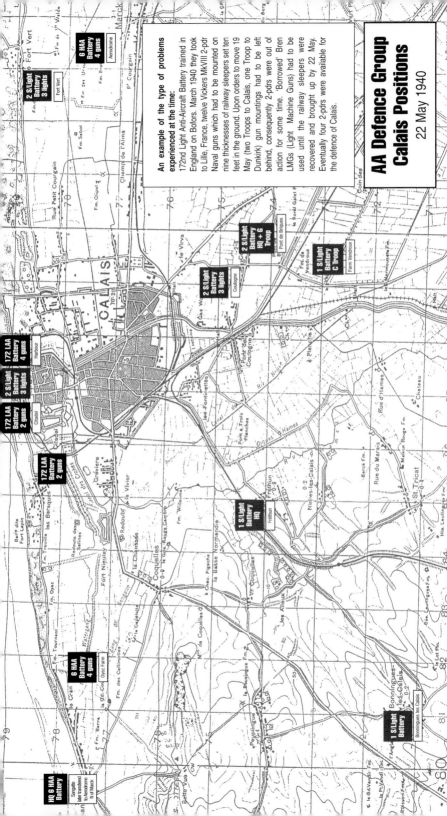

AA Defence Group
Calais Positions
22 May 1940

An example of the type of problems experienced at the time:

172nd Light Anti-Aircraft Battery trained in England on Bofors. March 1940 they took to Lille, France, twelve Vickers MkVIII 2-pdr Naval guns which had to be mounted on nine thicknesses of railway sleepers set ten feet in the ground. Upon orders to move 19 May (two Troops) to Calais, one Troop to Dunkirk) gun mountings had to be left behind, consequently 2-pdrs were out of action for some time. 'Borrowed' Bren LMGs (Light Machine Guns) had to be used until the railway sleepers were recovered and brought up by 22 May. Eventually four 2-pdrs were available for the defence of Calais.

6 HAA Battery 4 guns

2 S/Light Battery 3 lights

2 S/Light Battery HQ + G Troop

2 S/Light Battery 3 lights

1 S/Light Battery C Troop

172 LAA Battery 4 guns

2 S/Light Battery 3 lights

172 LAA Battery 2 guns

172 LAA Battery 2 guns

1 S/Light Battery HQ

6 HAA Battery 4 guns

1 S/Light Battery

HQ 6 HAA Battery

Sangatte itself to secure the submarine cable link to England. Oyez Farm was not an enviable site for a block as it was in open country with no obvious natural anti-tank obstacles, however a withdrawal to the line of the ramparts to the west of the Citadel would have exposed the four 3.7 inch guns of the Troop of 6 HAA Battery which had deployed behind Oyez Farm from 19 May. This Troop was well sited for anti-tank defence, both to its front facing down the road to Sangatte and half left with good visibility over the level ground between Sangatte up ahead and Coquelles to the south. Two of its guns were sited for this purpose whilst the other two were deployed to engage aircraft coming in low over the dunes at fifty feet to drop mines. An observation post was established in the dunes to direct the fire of these guns which could not see their targets at such a low level.

'C' Company were covering the eastern approaches to the town from Dunkirk and Gravelines on a line approximating a road which ran north – south, one kilometre beyond and roughly parallel to the eastern ramparts. Austin-Brown set up his HQ in a farm a little over one and a half kilometres east of the Pont de Gravelines and to the north of the Canal de Marck.

With the coming of the dawn Lieutenant Colonel Ellison-MacCartney found that Les Fontinettes was by no means the best possible site for battalion HQ so he moved to the Porte de Dunkerque just north of Bastion 5 at the eastern end of the Boulevard de l'Égalité. Likewise his company and platoon commanders began to reassess their hastily chosen positions of the previous evening and in several cases improvements began to be made. On the road to Fréthun 11 Platoon enlisted the help of the local stationmaster who agreed to shunt some railway trucks onto the nearby level crossing which ran on the far side of and parallel to the canal in addition to placing others to block the railway bridge over the canal itself.

2/Lieutenant Brewester's 12 platoon moved forward from their position at the crossroads of the Route de Coulogne and the Chemin de Grand Voyeau at the request of a RASC Major to take over a road block which consisted of a ten-ton truck which the Major had established 600 metres further down the road near Pont de Coulogne. Brewester was not happy with the position of the block when he arrived as he felt it would provide no advance warning of the approaching Germans so he retraced his steps to the crossroads taking the truck with him to improve his barricade.

A few miles to the east, however, some of the men of the 1st and 2nd Batteries of the 1st Searchlight Regiment who, even now were moving from their isolated outlying posts to concentrate on their Troop headquarters, following an order from Colonel Goldney, would find 23 May a day they would never forget.

Dawn of 23 May also saw the tanks of 3RTR concentrating in their designated assembly areas. The *Christchurch* had appeared at 4 o'clock the previous afternoon at approximately the same time as Lieutenant Colonel Keller had returned to the Gare Maritime and the unloading had gone on at the same snail's pace as that of QVR. As darkness fell unloading had still been in full swing. Already lacking one good night's sleep the tank men had worked on into another. Smoking was forbidden as the 4 gallon cans of petrol had been unloaded from the floating firebomb and stored on the quay. Sergeant Bill Close and the men of the reconnaissance troop had had good cause to thank their lucky stars that they drove two-man Daimler Dingo scout cars as they had watched some of their comrades rubbing the thick mineral jelly from their A9 cruisers with a fistful of greasy rags. The unloading had gone on all night mercifully uninterrupted by the Luftwaffe as the men had rummaged in the holds for missing gun barrels, machine gun mountings, high explosive shells and wireless components. Many of these missing items were never located. The first hint that there was a disturbing lack of communication on the part of the higher authorities had come an hour after the unloading of the *Christchurch* had at last got under way. Keller had returned to the harbour to supervise the unloading of the ship in the knowledge that his orders would come direct from GHQ at Hazebrouck, forty miles to the south-east, but the arrival, at around 5pm, of the Adjutant General, Lieutenant General Brownrigg, accompanied by General Lloyd, had only succeeded in confusing the issue. Brownrigg, on his way back to Dover after having evacuated the Rear HQ of the BEF from Wimereux, had repeated the view that only a small and lightly armoured German force was in the area and that Keller's over-riding priority was to advance to Boulogne and get in touch with 20 Guards Brigade in order to help secure the town. Keller had been told to get his tanks into the Forêt de Boulogne as soon as they were unloaded and ready to move. It was just as well that the tanks were still safely in the belly of the *Christchurch* at that moment for as Keller had listened to Brownrigg's orders 2 Panzer Division had commenced their assault on Boulogne and the leading elements of 1 Panzer Division after turning east, were at that very moment driving towards their overnight positions – in the Forêt de Boulogne!

As Keller digested these latest orders and kept an eye on the unloading he had reached the conclusion that the battalion would not be ready to move until after 6pm the following day if he were to be thoroughly prepared. Nevertheless, Brownrigg's orders had persuaded Keller that he should move out along the road to Boulogne. With this in mind he had gone out with his Adjutant, Captain George Moss, to recconnoitre the route to the west.

> *'Most of the available cover was occupied by the French troops but I eventually decided to concentrate at La Beussingue Farm and when this area was too congested, to concentrate other squadrons in the Coquelles area.'*

When Keller returned to the docks area to issue orders for the concentration he had found the area becoming congested with troops from a variety of regiments who had fallen back on Calais. Keller's tanks were being unloaded haphazardly and made ready for action, and such was the urgency to get them away from the dockside that as soon as they were deemed ready they were manned with whomever was available. Some of the Squadron Commanders did not get their own tanks and in some cases not even their own crews with the result that many machines were destined to go into action with crews who had never trained together. Corporal Alan Woolaston of 'C' Squadron had been standing at the dockside when the *Christchurch* was being unloaded.

'When we were assigned to tanks in Calais, my tank commander was Lieutenant Ginger Moir… but it was a piecemeal operation. We were stood along the dockside, the tanks came off the ship and it was a case of "gunner – you; driver – you; commander – you,"… I think it was a matter of luck whether you became a cruiser or a light tank crew. I was put on an A13 as gunner and the driver was a chap called 'Tich' Newman.' TANK MUSEUM

The first of the Mark VI 'B' light tanks to come ashore had been ordered to take up covering positions around the docks and Keller urged his Squadron Commanders to begin the journey to their chosen 'harbour' area near Vieux Coquelles with their 'scratch' squadrons as soon as they were ready to move.

Mark VI light tanks in action in France 1940.

CHAPTER FIVE

COOK THE DUCKS FOR DINNER

The Green Jacket Battalions which followed 1QVR and 3RTR into Calais to complete 30 Brigade on the afternoon of 23 May were much stronger and better equipped than their territorial cousin. 1RB and 2KRRC were both regular battalions from regiments with a proud military pedigree. Their ranks were filled with experienced men like Rifleman Don Gurr and reservists who had seen many years service in the pre-war Army. At the age of thirty-nine Don Gurr had already served in the RB for twenty-one years. Under normal circumstances he would have retired with a pension in the April of 1940, but the war had put a stop to that. He was a dispatch rider (DR) with 'A' Company HQ section and came under the orders of its company commander Major John Taylor, and had taken nineteen year old Doug Wheeler under his wing. Although the Rifle Brigade was Doug Wheeler's life, youngsters like him were in the minority in both 1RB and 2KRRC. It was largely due to the experience of the 'old sweats' and their skills in the finest traditions of the Rifle Regiments that Calais was held for as

Rifleman Don Gurr, probably the finest shot in the British Army.

long as it was. Paradoxically they were the very men that the British Army and Churchill could ill afford to lose at that crucial stage of the war.

The first battalion to arrive was 2KRRC aboard the cross-channel steamer, the SS *Royal Daffodil*, with 1RB and Brigadier Nicholson and his

The Green Jackets of 2KRRC arrived on the *Royal Daffodil*. Her sister ship *The Royal Sovereign* is seen here berthed at the Gare Maritime, Calais.

Brigade HQ following aboard the SS *Archangel*. 1RB and 2KRRC had become the two infantry battalions of 30 Brigade when it had been formed at Tidworth on 20 April for service in Norway. They were the only two mechanized infantry battalions (officially known as Motor Battalions), of 1 Armoured Division, the only British Armoured Division then in existence. The move to Norway never materialized but as the notion of using Calais as a port of supply gained favour at the War Office, the two motor battalions wee deemed eminently suitable for the roving commission of escorting convoys from Calais to the BEF in the field through a landscape then thought to be inhabited by 'light' German forces.

The motor battalions each had a roll of about 750. A rifle section plus a corporal or sergeant and a driver were carried in a 15cwt Morris Commercial truck. Four trucks made up a motor platoon. Each company had its own scout platoon mounted in Bren gun carriers and each battalion had its own support company including two machine gun platoons, a mortar and anti-tank platoons. This gave the motor battalions more firepower then conventional infantry battalions even though there were fewer riflemen. Another difference was the use of wireless down to the level of junior officers which influenced their tactical deployment. It is ironic that the men who established the principles of the use of motor battalions between 1937 and 1940 never had the opportunity to act on them at Calais.

2 KRRC had left Fornham Park a little before midnight on 21 May Twenty-one year old 2/Lieutenant Grismond Davies-Scourfield was in

Rifleman Roach at the wheel of one of 1 RB's 15-cwt Morris-Commercials. He was wounded and managed to escape from Calais before it fell.

command of the scout platoon of 'B' Company. His command consisted of three sections mounted in lightly armoured Bren gun carriers each armed with light machine guns and a Boys anti-tank rifle. There were about forty men in all.

The battalion drove through the night in a deluge of rain, which soaked the men to the skin. They skirted London and took the Great West Road where the vehicles were directed into a petrol station to fill up by their Adjutant Captain Alick Williams. Here some of the young officers used the opportunity to make a last contact with their families. 2/Lieutenant Philip Pardoe, in command of 'C' Company scout platoon, managed to get a telegram off to his parents. **'Cook the ducks for dinner'**, it read. It was the family's pre-arranged code for, 'We're going overseas.'

Whilst the officers contacted their families the men chatted to each other about their call to active service. Two of Davies-Scourfield's platoon, Corporal Bill Gorringe, twenty-seven and twenty year old Corporal Ron Savage were travelling together and Ron Savage recalled their conversation.

'Bill said, "I'm not very keen on going Ron. I wish it was in another six months." I said "Why? That's what we're here for." But he wasn't scared. He'd married a girl while we were training at Stalbridge and he told me she was pregnant. He only wanted to stay to see the baby born.'

The battalion came to a halt on the outskirts of Southampton at around 10 am on the morning of 22 May, and as soon as they stopped their vehicles had been seized by '...somewhat excited staff officers.' Davies-Scourfield recalls that,

'In Southampton staff officers relieved us of all maps and stuck labels on the vehicles. We moved on and halted under some trees close to the High Street: here more staff officers ordered us to dismount and remove all personal kit which would then be driven to the docks for loading onto ships. I decided I would be more usefully employed at the docks than waiting with the Battalion..., leaving the rest of the platoon under Sergeant Wall, I proceeded with the drivers. I spent the rest of the day trying to get my carriers on the vehicle ship. It was a lengthy and trying business, mainly because of the continual orders and counter-orders from the embarkation staff.'

Ron Savage

Embarkation turned into a complete fiasco as the entreaties of Lieutenant Colonel Miller and his officers were brushed aside by staff officers who appeared to be ignorant of the composition and functions of a motor battalion. He was not allowed to arrange anything. All he received were, '... a lot of vague instructions from half a dozen different people.' The result was '...considerable muddle and confusion.'

1RB had arrived in Southampton at midday after a similarly trying journey through the night from Needham Market in Suffolk during which Don Gurr had made a detour on his motorcycle to see his sister Margaret who lived near East Grinstead. Margaret Bishop would not see her brother for another five years.

The experiences of 2KRRC were repeated when the Rifle Brigade's turn came to load up. Rifleman Roy Archer was detailed to see that the transport was loaded properly.

> 'All the vehicles were lined up on the quayside and the petrol was pumped out of all the trucks and Bren carriers. I was horrified to see how the stevedores 'shovelled' our trucks into the holds like a load of scrap. I protested to the foreman who said, " can't kid-glove 'em mate, we are to get the ship away as soon as possible." There appeared to be too many foremen and not enough workers, but we did get away in the end.'

After supervising the loading of his carriers 2/Lieutenant Davies-Scourfield had made his way towards the quay where the *Royal Daffodil* waited with it gangways down for the rest of his battalion. A short while later his own battalion marched into view with Colonel Miller at its head. Davies-Scourfield joined the men as they filed up the gangways. It was now 7pm and the convoy of two personnel and two vehicle ships cast off and steamed into Southampton Water en-route for Dover and then Calais. No one cheered them off. Major Jack Poole commanding 'B' Company could not help but draw comparisons with the patriotic send off he had had twenty-five years before as a young subaltern with 4 KRRC on his way to 'the war to end wars.'

Looking out over the side of the ship 2/Lieutenant Davies-Scourfield could not get the words of an embarkation officer out of his head. He had

Second Lieutenant Davies-Scourfield (seated) with some of 5 Platoon, B Company, 2 KRRC in 1939. With him is his wireless operator.

met the NCO earlier on the quay and noticing the uniform of his own regiment had immediately engaged him in conversation.

'" I suppose you're pretty busy just now." I remarked chattily, " plenty of people sailing and all that."

"Not many sailing" he replied and, lowering his voice, added "but there'll be plenty coming home. The regiment's going the wrong way if you ask me."'

After putting in at Dover, where Brigadier Nicholson was told that his two regular battalions would act offensively with 3RTR to relieve Boulogne, the convoy sailed to Calais. A further ship, the *Autocarrier*, joined the convoy at Dover carrying only eight of the twelve guns of 229 Anti-Tank Battery, 58 Anti-Tank Regiment, 49 Division. There had not been space to embark the full complement, the *Autocarrier* already having vehicles on board. Captain Woodley, their CO, was ordered to embark only two of his Troops, the rest, he was told would follow twelve hours later. They would never arrive. On their arrival the eight guns of 229 AT Battery took up positions on all the main routes into Calais.

The information given to Brigadier Nicholson, such as it was, was now passed to Lieutenant Colonel Miller and the CO of 1RB, Lieutenant Colonel Chandos Hoskyns. He informed them that on landing their battalions would move first to dispersal areas in the dunes, 1RB to the north and 2KRRC to the south of the Bassin des Chasses, and then to positions roughly to the right and left of the Calais-Boulogne road. The first battalion to disembark would hold the right of the road. The information was then filtered down to the junior officers. On board the *Royal Daffodil* Major Poole summoned his last platoon commanders' conference and issued some sort of maps. He told them that weak German units were feeling their way towards Calais and that 2KRRC and 1RB would support the troops already there.

Aboard the *Archangel* conferences were also taking place. Doug Wheeler, in his role as DR, escorted 'A' Company officers onto the top deck for a meeting with Major Taylor and he was able to eavesdrop on what was said.

'He told us that a small mobile armoured unit was creating havoc behind the lines in Northern France and we had the task of locating and destroying it. This was exactly the job for which the 1st Armoured Division had been created and trained for being a fully mobile unit.'

The journey across the Channel was eventful and at least two bombs were dropped on the convoy, just missing the lone destroyer escort and landing just aft of

Doug Wheeler

the *Archangel*. The coast of France came into view and as the *Royal Daffodil* neared Calais, Lieutenant Colonel Miller heard the sound of gunfire getting louder. Soon the *Royal Daffodil* was nosing into the harbour followed closely by the *Archangel*. The scenes in the harbour as the riflemen moved off to their dispersal areas, was not what some of the younger soldiers expected. As 1RB began to disembark Doug Wheeler was surprised that the docks were 'in a mess' and was struck by the 'equipment and soldiers and other people all over the place.' Charles Green also in A Company 1RB saw his first casualties on the dockside.

Charles Green

'*We went by the railway station from the pier and all the stretcher cases were there. If you've ever seen the film* Gone With the Wind, *in Atlanta with all those bodies?, well that's what it was like. Not as many but there were a lot covered up. There were a lot of seriously wounded Every time an air raid came everybody would scatter except us! They said that the stevedores kept running off every time there was an air raid. Of course, it was only natural, they were civilians. We knew we were in it when they started shelling the pier.*'

There was precious little by way of help in unloading equipment. Rifleman Thomas Sandford of 'A' Company 2KRRC began to unload the ammunition which had been dumped aboard the *Royal Daffodil* by the embarkation staff at Southampton along with his colleagues. Corporal Jones of 2 platoon began to break open the boxes and dole out linen bandoliers of .303 SAA in clips of five rounds. These were slung around the necks of the riflemen until the weight bent them almost double. Some wag remarked that they looked more like Mexican bandits instead of British soldiers. Both battalions moved to their 'hide' areas in the sand dunes near the Bassin des Chasses in the pouring rain to await the arrival of their vehicle ships, which turned up an hour and a half later but could not berth due to a low tide. It was not until around 5pm that unloading proper could begin. In the meantime the battalion commanders issued their orders for the deployment of their troops in line with Brigadier Nicholson's instructions which he had issued an hour earlier.

Brigadier Nicholson was faced with a welter of conflicting orders and reports during the next few hours and after his first reconnaissance mission he decided that his small force could not possibly be used in an offensive capacity to relieve Boulogne as General Brownrigg had ordered. The tanks of 3RTR would come into contact with the German Panzers near Guines later that afternoon as would the Searchlights near Les Attaques and Coulogne. Nicholson began to realize that the defence of Calais was becoming a matter of urgency and studying his maps he determined to hold the heart shaped outer perimeter of approximately 12 kilometres formed by the nineteenth century ramparts and moat and block all approaches with his regular troops. 1QVR and 3RTR were already blocking routes beyond the line of the ramparts and he saw little value in exposing his small force further by sending the Green Jackets into the surrounding countryside. If this line became untenable then an inner perimeter formed by the canals and waterways around the Old Town would be taken up. He received another order, however, which, he was told, was to be given priority 'overriding all other considerations', even as his troops were coming ashore, to send a sizable portion of 1RB to accompany a convoy of 10-ton trucks loaded with 350,000 rations to Dunkirk. Nicholson was not offered reinforcements for this venture even though it was obvious that his brigade would have to defend Calais. He was left with no alternative but to order the loading of the ten-ton lorries for the rations' run.

2KRRC had been first ashore and were ordered to deploy along the western and south-western faces of the outer perimeter from the coast to the banks of the Canal de Calais, mid-way between Bastions 6 and 7 and their junction with 1RB. From the dispersal area 'B' Company 2KRRC under Major Jack Poole were ordered to take up a position in the centre of 2KRRC's front on the line of the ramparts from a point on the railway south of Bastion 10 as far as Bastion 9. When Poole arrived he deployed his platoons astride the main Calais-Boulogne road west of the Pont Jourdan bridge. To the right 'C' Company under Captain Maurice Johnson held the line from the railway as far as the seafront near Bastion 11, a difficult area to defend with numerous canal and railway bridges criss-crossing their position. Johnson spread his platoons to cover the ramparts and all the approaches and crossing points, establishing an advance post to cover the rail crossing just south of the Cimetière Nord. On 'B' Company's left and up to the Canal de Calais was 'D' Company under Major Lord Godfrey Cromwell. 'A' Company under Major Derek Trotter was in reserve but was initially ordered to hold the line of the eastern ramparts until the companies of 1RB arrived. They helped in strengthening the barricade of two single deck tram cars in the Rue Mollien near the Pont de Gravelines, already begun by men of 1QVR.

Jack Poole Captured 10 May 1915 near Ypres he was to become a PoW for the second time at Calais.

Rifleman Thomas Sandford and his comrades took up position on top of the ramparts, mixing with riflemen of 1QVR whose chaplain the Rev R G Heard was moving among them ladling out tea from a large jug. The barricade in the Rue Mollien was strengthened with large stones from a nearby stonemason's yard in which Sandford spied an open top vintage car. Calling his mates they pushed the car out of the yard and along the Rue Mollien. A Rifleman sat behind the wheel and hooted the horn as the old car gathered speed and the rest of them jumped on the running board, pursued by a French civilian, presumably the owner, shouting and waving his arms in the air. With a heave the riflemen turned the car over at the barricade to a roar from the growing civilian audience. The 'owner' finally caught up threw his beret on the floor and jumped on it in exasperation.

Thomas Sandford

As the evening of the 23rd May drew on Lieutenant Colonel Hoskyns in his HQ at Bastion 2 gave orders for several platoons to reinforce QVR positions on the outer perimeter to the east and south-east. 'A' and 'I' Companies under Major John Taylor and Major Peter Brush were ordered to concentrate to the north of the Calais - Dunkirk Road prior to patrolling the route for some twelve miles ahead of the rations convoy escort, a task for which the carriers of 'B' Company, (Major Arthur Hamilton-Russell, known throughout the regiment as 'The Boy') had been selected with support from five tanks of 3RTR. If they had moved immediately they may have had some chance of success but it took many hours for the column to get organized, due to the slow unloading of RB vehicles and the lack of enthusiasm on the part of Lieutenant Colonel Keller to commit his tanks before first light. In any case Keller had had problems of his own whilst IRB were attempting to equip the rations escort.

As darkness fell Rifleman Sandford made his way back on top of the flat-topped rampart to await the arrival of the riflemen of 1RB. Looking east he could see a fierce red glow in the direction of Dunkirk and about three miles away the bonfires of the units of 1 Panzer Division signalling the limits of their advance to the Luftwaffe. Listening to the whine of shells as they passed overhead towards the docks the men waited for the dawn. The 24 May would be Empire Day and whilst Sandford's battle was about to begin, that of 3RTR had already started.

Original sketch map of initial positions of B Company, 2KRRC, around Bastion 9 drawn by Major Jack Poole. IWM 91/8/1

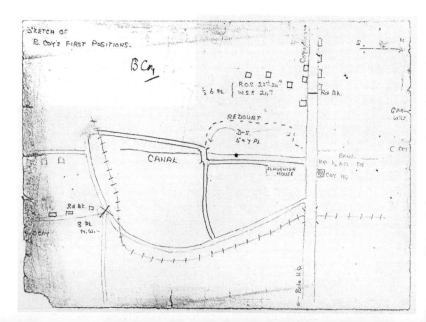

CHAPTER SIX

I'M TRYING TO FIGHT A BLOODY BATTLE

Whilst the two Green Jacket battalions of 30 Brigade were disembarking and preparing to move to their allotted positions on the Outer Perimeter the battle for Calais began in earnest in the countryside beyond.

By the time Nicholson and his two regular battalions had landed in Calais Lieutenant Colonel Keller of 3RTR was still without his full complement of tanks and equipment. He had also been subject to a rash of apparently conflicting instructions. He had been under the impression that he was to advance towards Boulogne but at 11pm the previous evening an officer had arrived by car claiming to be Major Bailey of the Ox and Bucks Light Infantry, serving as a liaison officer with GHQ in Hazebrouck. He had given verbal orders for Keller to move south and take possession of the bridges over the Aa Canal at St. Omer and Watten in order to help relieve the pressure on Gort's HQ which was in danger of being trapped by the German advance towards St. Omer. This latest twist had been the third order to be received by Keller in less than twelve hours and had been in direct conflict to those issued at 5 pm on 22 May by Lieutenant General Brownrigg at the dockside. These latest orders would send his unit in almost the opposite direction from the one he believed he was to take. If the

British tank men of the 3 Royal Tank Regiment. Corporal, later Sergeant, Bill Close is standing on the left.

orders were genuine it also meant that not only were the Germans near Boulogne, they were also driving towards St.Omer. Even the most cursory glance at a map would reveal that the Calais garrison was being encircled to the south. With this in mind and being aware of growing rumours of 'Fifth Columnists' and German infiltrators in Calais, Keller had been understandably wary and had '..grave doubts of identity'. He was only convinced when Colonel Holland had vouched for the credentials of Major Bailey personally.

In response to Major Bailey's request Colonel Keller had issued orders to Major Simpson commanding 'A' Squadron to send out a patrol.

'Just before dark I was ordered to send a patrol to St.Omer. This consisted of Second Lieutenant Mundy with No 2 Troop. I also detailed a patrol of three light tanks under Second Lieutenant Paul to report to the CO. These patrols moved off under orders of the CO and I proceeded with all the remaining light tanks and scout cars that were off the ship to La Beussingue Farm. Second Lieutenant Mundy's patrol got through to St.Omer and rejoined about 0400 hrs 23.5.40. Second Lieutenant Paul's troop rejoined just before that and tanks gradually came out from Calais in driblets as they came off the ship.'

The patrol of three light tanks under 2 /Lieutenant Mundy had set out

British soldiers pass an Infantry Tank Mark I Matilda as they withdraw towards the French coast, May 1940.

around 1 am 23 May along the Ardres road and returned unscathed with the news that St. Omer was for the moment free of German troops but was being heavily shelled and lit by the flames from burning buildings. At 3 am, two hours after he had sent out his patrol towards St. Omer, Keller had received a coded signal from General Brownrigg, by then safely back in Dover, confirming his earlier order for Keller to advance to Boulogne!

By daybreak more and more tanks were joining those already assembled near Vieux Coquelles and Major Bailey, who saw Keller again that morning and was of the opinion that Second Lieutenant Mundy's patrol could not possibly have made it through to St. Omer, had once more urged Keller to try and get his force through to assist GHQ in spite of Brownrigg's latest signal to the contrary. Bailey had insisted that orders direct from GHQ must take priority over all others and as he himself wished to return to GHQ he had asked for an escort both to protect his staff car and to make contact with Lord Gort's HQ. Keller again issued orders to Major Simpson.

'About 0800 hrs I received orders to send a light tank troop to escort Major Bailey (GHQ) to St. Omer where he believed GHQ to be. I ordered 2/Lieutenant Eastman with No 3 Troop consisting of three light tanks to do this. About half an hour after they moved off I received a wireless message from Second Lieutenant Eastman to say they didn't know where Major Bailey had got to and asked me what to do. I told him if he could not find Major Bailey at once, to proceed on to St.Omer and get in touch with GHQ which I understood from Major Bailey was essential in order to report the situation. I informed my CO that I had done this. About half an hour after this Major Bailey turned up, having taken the wrong road and been wounded.'

Eastman's patrol had run into heavy opposition five kilometres south of Ardres and only one British tank had managed to escape the German noose and had eventually made it back to the area of Coquelles.

When Major Bailey eventually turned up wounded at Keller's HQ at La Beussingue Farm, his car bore the bullet holes gained so recently in his encounter with the Germans. He had run across a German motor cycle patrol near Les Cappes after taking a wrong turn off the main road a little way south-east of Les Attaques and had lost contact with Eastman's tanks but he had managed to get away. In spite of his narrow escape he reiterated his earlier demands that Keller should send his tanks to secure the bridges over the St. Omer Canal. Keller was not convinced as to the wisdom of such a move. By noon five of his tanks, two Mark VI and three Cruisers, were still being unloaded from the *Christchurch* at the Calais quay-side under the direction of Keller's second in command, Major Mahoney. Two more of his tanks had been lost south of Ardres in the aborted quest to escort Major Bailey to GHQ, an action which confirmed

British A9 tank in service with 3 RTR. It had a 40mm gun and three .303 machine guns and carried a crew of six.

that German forces were advancing on Calais from the south-east. He had also received reports of another German column moving from the south-west.

> *'All the morning while at my HQ a constant stream of French officers were coming to me and asking for help against a German column advancing NE from the direction of Marquise. I had to refuse as I was not ready and I also informed them that I was under special GHQ orders. They were very indignant.'*

This column was the leading edge of 1 Panzer Division under Oberst Kruger, heading north-east towards Gravelines.

By 12.30 pm Keller, unsure of the exact location of the German columns, had reached a decision very much against his better judgment. He would try to get through to St. Omer and thence to Hazebrouck with all available machines hoping that he could pass ahead of Kruger's column before it reached the vicinity of Guines. He had ordered squadrons to be made up equally from what he had available and the men had busied themselves in preparing to move off. The hotchpotch nature of forming squadrons out of the tanks available was evident in Major Simpson's command. In theory he was the commanding officer of 'A' Squadron but he would go into action with a composite squadron of nine tanks in three Troops made up of men and machines from 'A' 'B' and 'C' Squadrons.

Captain Barry O'Sullivan had only been with the battalion a few days since his return from service in India, on top of which he had changed squadrons only the day before they left England so he knew none of the crew of his Cruiser properly. He was now second in command of 'B' Squadron and was preparing his tank for action in spite of the obvious problems he was facing. He had no high explosive rounds for his 3.7 inch mortar and, like Major Simpson, was having trouble with his two front machine guns which would not fit properly into their mountings. He had only managed to acquire the machine-guns at the very last minute as anxious tank men continued to scrabble around the holds of the *Christchurch* for guns and ammunition. Hasty improvisations were made so that the guns could at least be fired from the tanks.

The battalion, minus the transport of 'B' echelon and the five tanks still in Calais with Captain R H Howe, was as ready as it ever would be by 2pm and shortly afterwards the column set out in drizzling rain south-east along the road towards Guines via Vieux Coquelles and St. Tricat. They were led by a troop of three light tanks under the command of Major Reeves of 'B' Squadron which formed 'protection front'. They made slow progress pushing against columns of French army lorries, marching troops and refugees.

'We were almost completely disorganized when the advance to St.Omer started... The route lay through a small village called Hames Boucres about four miles along the road in a dip between two ridges of undulating hills.
'B' Squadron was leading and the advance guard troops, about five hundred yards in front of the Squadron, soon reported that they had passed through and were nearing the crest of the hill on the south side of the village.'

In the wake of the leading vehicles came the rest of 'B' Squadron; three cruisers followed by Major Reeves and Squadron HQ in two A9's and then the remainder of the tanks. Keller's tank serving as Battalion HQ came next in front of 'C' Squadron with 'A' Squadron in reserve bringing up the rear. 'C' Squadron had initially been deployed as right flank guard but due to a warren of sunken roads and the proximity of the railway to the road, it was called in and ordered to 'shake out' after successfully negotiating the 'bottleneck' at St. Tricat.

Out in front, 'B' Squadron's first task was to reconnoitre the crossings over the Canal de Calais at Guines and gain any information as to the strength of German armoured forces operating in the area. They had not gone far after passing through St. Tricat when two German light tanks were sighted on the right flank some one and a half kilometres away. 'C' Squadron received the order 'Protection Right' and the German tanks withdrew.

Sergeant Jimmy Cornwell was in the leading Mark VI of the advance guard. He had led the battalion out past the windmill on the slopes of la Pente de Moulin, or 'Windmill Hill' a little less than three kilometres south-west of Vieux Coquelles, and had driven on for more than three kilometres until his tank had entered a sunken road. Now he was sure that he saw movements on the high ground ahead about a mile to his right front. At that distance there was no way of knowing what it could be and the mass movements of refugees had also clouded the issue so Sergeant Cornwell stopped his tank and climbed up the bank into the hedgerow to take a closer look through his binoculars.

A little way behind Major Reeves and providing close support in his A9 was Captain O'Sullivan. He sighted what appeared to be a large mechanized force advancing up the main road towards Calais.

'In my immediate view, at about 1,000 yards, there appeared to be seven to eight enemy tanks armed with the equivalent to our 2-pounder and accompanied by three lorries; the remainder of the force being hidden from our view by woods. On our mutual encounter, both forces appeared to hesitate for some seconds before opening fire. The German tanks were halted on the road and all in position behind trees. We were deployed on the fields and advancing towards them.'

Over his radio Major Simpson received confirmation of the contact.

'When I was roughly about St. Tricat I heard B sqn reporting enemy armoured cars and light tanks. I then realized we must have run into a fairly large column. I was called to come on and get my tanks into action. I went on and got into action on the road running SW from Hames Boucres.'

Keller's report on the action compiled later was very specific with regard to the location of the Germans when they were first sighted.

'My advance guard after passing about 1 mile SE of Hames Boucres reported a column halted on the road to the south. This road ran from Pihen-les-Guines to Guines. The sqn cmdr said he did not know whether it was French or German. It was raining at the time and the visibility was very bad. I went forward with my HQ but was unable to tell what it was. Eventually my 2i/c saw men removing a/T guns from the lorries so I ordered fire to be opened and the battle commenced.'

A German column deploys as it comes under fire.

The hesitation in identifying the German column was completely understandable given the prevailing weather conditions, the state of the roads, choked as they were with columns of civilian refugees and the fact that neither the British nor Germans were expecting to meet such large armoured forces in the Calais area. Second Lieutenant Quentin Carpendale, also in the advance guard, was another who witnessed an armoured column sheltering under some trees but due to the mist and drizzle was unable to make out whether they were French or German. Carpendale upright in his turret, left the road and moved his Troop across open country to investigate, advancing on the column which was stationary and resting. Carpendale got to within twenty yards of the column before he realized they were Germans. He seemed to feel that the men under the trees were as surprised to see him as he was to see them. A German officer fired a revolver at Carpendale's head as he turned in his tracks to escape.

Major Reeves noticed that Germans swung into action quickly once they had established that the tanks driving towards them were hostile.

> 'It was very impressive to see the reaction of the German column on being attacked. They very rapidly dismounted from their vehicles and got their anti-tank guns into action, and soon shots were whizzing past our ears.'

Sergeant Cornwell was still in the hedge trying to make out what he had seen up ahead when the A13 Cruiser belonging to the Adjutant rumbled past him down the road. It had not gone far when Cornwell picked up muzzle flashes from the hedgerows he had been scrutinizing. He knew instantly that they had made their first real contact with German tanks, '...nicely hull-down and wondering what a battalion of British tanks was doing heading towards them as if they were out for a drive in the country.' The German fire hit the Adjutant's A13 which became the battalion's first battle casualty.

The battle which followed lasted some three-quarters of an hour. It was a confused, chaotic and rambling affair in the open fields and on the bye-roads and tracks between the village of Hames-Boucres and a little way beyond what, in 1940, was known as Grand St. Blaise, and which is now the site of la Waille Ferme, one kilometre down the road to the south-west. Captain O'Sullivan found that the Germans were in greater strength than had at first been anticipated and that they could bring greater fire power to bear.

> 'From the start the enemy were able to concentrate superior fire power on us, as there appeared to be only three or four of our cruisers up, who could reply with any effect. We concentrated our machine guns on the lorries. Except for distracting the attention of the enemy, our light tanks were naturally ineffective, and we were forced to withdraw back over the

crest of the hill, having knocked out the lorries and two of the German heavy cruisers and two light tanks.'

The effect of concentrating fire on the lorries and rendering them *hors de combat* effectively blocked the road for the duration of the battle, preventing further forward movement. Sergeant Cornwell drove out of the sunken road towards the Germans making use of whatever cover he could find and intended to take a shot but when he tried to locate other British tanks he found that they, like Captain O'Sullivan, were in the process of withdrawing in the general direction of 'Windmill Hill', some machines putting down a smoke screen as cover.

Two of the tanks which were attempting to put down a smoke screen as they withdrew belonged to two squadron commanders, Major Simpson and Major Reeves, and they had both been frustrated by their lack of firepower in the battle thus far.

'I could do nothing with my tank as I had only one effective MG and a smoke mortar. I then received orders to withdraw and I attempted to put down a smoke screen to cover our withdrawal but it was useless as there was no wind and the smoke pillared straight into the air.

'My own tank was a cruiser type A9, which had only a smoke Howitzer and one MG on it. This was not encouraging, as I could only watch other tanks fighting and not hit back myself. Soon one tank after another was put out of action. It was obvious that we were out-gunned and out-numbered, and the only thing was a withdrawal back to Calais. My tank would at least put down smoke so with its help, and the help of two other 'smoke tanks', we put down a smoke screen and withdrew to a ridge between Coquelles and Calais.'

Watching the battle unfold from his Dingo reconnaissance car Sergeant Bill Close had noticed that initially the fire of the British cruisers with their 2-pounder guns had been accurate and had kept the panzers at bay until the Germans had deployed their anti-tank guns and field artillery, at which point the initial successes evaporated. An increasing fusilade of shells and bullets then began to whistle through the air prompting Sergeant Close to move nearer to Lieutenant Colonel Keller's cruiser, 200 metres away from Captain O'Sullivan back down the road behind the crest of a hill. No sooner had Close begun to move towards the tank for shelter when a shell exploded on Keller's turret jamming the gun but otherwise not interfering with the machine's mobility.

200 metres ahead O'Sullivan's tank was also under fire and was hit twice by 2-pounder shells which smashed part of the off-side suspension and track. In spite of that he managed to swing broadside to the Germans and crawled down a bank in a well camouflaged, hull-down position. O'Sullivan looked out to assess the damage and saw that,

'the suspension was damaged beyond repair, and that the track was

some seventy yards away. The tank had also settled into the marshy ground. As the wireless was out of order owing to a broken part, I ordered the crew to keep the lorries under fire whilst I went over to see Colonel Keller...to find out what he intended to do. I was informed that a right flank attack was intended and that a light tank section was coming over to join me in trying to distract the enemy's attention and contain him during the manoeuvre.'

Keller, well aware that the Germans were gaining the upper hand with the use of their field artillery, hoped that, by withdrawing to a position behind the railway line which ran south-west from Calais via Fréthun and looped west almost encircling Pihen-les-Guines, he could re-group and mount a further attack from the south. Major Simpson was ordered to rally on the east of the road behind the railway line so he began to collect his tanks together. Keller then ordered 'A' and 'C' Squadrons to deploy to the right with the intention of outflanking the German force, whilst the task of diverting their attention and holding them with frontal fire went to 'B' Squadron. As Keller had promised, two light tanks and a cruiser appeared to join O' Sullivan, and the cruiser succeeded in disabling one of the German machines before it and the two light tanks were knocked out themselves a few minutes later by concentrated and accurate fire from anti-tank guns and the guns of the German tanks. O'Sullivan, without high explosive mortar shells, only had his machine guns with

Lieutenant Colonel Keller

which to draw the Germans' attention. For ten minutes after seeing Colonel Keller he continued to fire until the off-side front turret machine gun was hit twice in quick succession and put out of action, badly wounding the gunner, Trooper Brown in the process. Meanwhile Troopers Galbraith and Price were firing the machine gun which was co-axially mounted with the mortar in the tank. O'Sullivan himself was busy manhandling the third machine gun on to the top of the tank as the direct hit had rendered it useless in its original position. For a further five minutes O'Sullivan fired from the top of the tank until he noticed German troops who had moved into position through trees on either side of him some 500 metres away. They opened up with anti-tank guns at which point O'Sullivan dismounted the gun and made for a gap in the fence some twelve metres from the tank to try to dislodge them.

Elsewhere on the battlefield radio traffic was spilling over into some of the tanks which had been 'netted' successfully and the hoarse voice of Colonel Keller was heard to shout repeatedly at an unknown commander, 'Why aren't you firing at the bastards?'

The two light tanks which had been sent over to O'Sullivan earlier now

PzKmpf Mk IVs during the push to the coast.

appeared to be deserted and the A13 cruiser was on fire. A light tank under the command of Lieutenant Deuchar was in the open fifty metres away and was being hit repeatedly. It was now twenty minutes since O'Sullivan had spoken with Colonel Keller and he realized that there was little chance of the battalion reappearing. He judged by the ferocity of the shelling that they had met with heavy opposition on the right flank and had been forced to withdraw towards Calais. Two more shells thumped into his tank as he fired from the bank, fatally wounding Trooper Price and another crewman who were manning the smoke mortar and the nearby machine gun.

O'Sullivan reasoned that his men had drawn the fire of the Germans for a good half hour and had accomplished their task to the best of their ability. As the firing eased a little he decided that they could be of no further use in their present position as they were in danger of being isolated. He opted to make his way north in the direction of Calais with his four remaining crew members. Leaving the machine gun behind he began to move across country on foot with Trooper Brown who was badly hurt, and three young troopers, one of whom was in a state of shock.

O'Sullivan had decided to try to make his way back towards Calais. Colonel Keller had also reached a decision to order all his tanks to withdraw and rally on the ridge south-west of Coquelles about three miles from the centre of Calais. It was now near 4 pm and as Keller led his tanks back towards Coquelles a message crackled through on his wireless set. One of Keller's accounts of the incident is short and to the point,

> *'OC 'B' Echelon on air re a Brigadier Nicholson unknown to Comdr 3RTR thought to be fresh GHQ orders. Replied middle of battle what does he want – put on air. Nicholson refused to talk asked for map ref – given and stated would come to see comdr. This about 4.30p.m.'*

Keller had just lost four light and three cruiser tanks and was probably aware that that meant some of his men had been killed or captured and that some, like O'Sullivan's crew, were struggling back towards Calais. His battalion was still effectively under fire and he was in the process of attempting to salvage a difficult situation. He had been given numerous contradictory orders and was probably in no mood for more. He had no knowledge of Nicholson and was not aware that his battalion was now effectively under the Brigadier's command. Other accounts record that Keller's terse response was, **'Get off the air, I am trying to fight a bloody battle.'**

Brigadier Nicholson came on air again half an hour later and said he would come out personally to see Keller in Coquelles. Keller himself was aware that his battalion was still in a 'tank infested area' and Major Reeves, who had managed to make it back to the ridge south-west of Coquelles, could look down from that vantage point and see '...German columns slowly wending their way towards us at about three miles distance.'

It was only when Brigadier Nicholson arrived in his car to talk to Keller personally at 8 pm that the issue of the chain of command was finally resolved. He told Keller that he had recently landed to take charge of all

The Battle of Hames Boucres. A knocked out British Vickers Mk VIb Light Tank of 3RTR is being examined by some panzer crewmen on the road south of Hames Boucres. The smoke up the road is from two British tanks just north of the site of La Waille Farm. A British tank man's black beret can be seen on the floor beside the tank.

See Tour 3
page 171

British forces in Calais and that he had brought with him the staff of 30 Infantry Brigade and two regular Green Jacket battalions. During the meeting Nicholson gave orders for 3RTR to withdraw into Calais and to assemble in the Parc St. Pierre opposite the Hôtel de Ville after dark to refill with petrol in readiness to support an attempt to break out east on the Marck road towards Dunkirk with elements of 1RB. With this in mind Nicholson told Keller to wait on the Pont St. Pierre which bridged the Canal de Calais at the junction of Boulevard Lafayette and Boulevard de l'Égalité, until he came to see him again.

Nicholson then left in his car and was escorted by Sergeant Bill Close and his driver Billy Barlow in their Dingo back to the cellars of the Clinique in the Boulevard Leon Gambetta, where Nicholson's staff had joined that of Colonel Holland.

> *'We followed the Brigadier's car back to Calais. As we pulled away Billy Barlow...nodded towards three bundles covered by groundsheets. Boots stuck out from under them...*
>
> *"Who are they?"*
>
> *I couldn't say. As they were from tank crews we must both have known them...*
>
> *"What'll happen to them?"*
>
> *I wasn't sure. We'd never practised burying the dead during exercises on Salisbury Plain.'*

The tanks now began to arrive in Calais from the direction of Coquelles a

Confident of victory – 'young lions' of the Whermacht pause in the battle for France.

little after 9pm. They had left the ridge line just in time for a German plane had left a smoke trail over their position a short time before their departure and a little later the ridge was shelled.

One of the tanks which trundled into Calais that night was under the command of Major Reeves, although it wasn't the tank in which he had fought earlier that day.

'On approaching Calais my tank broke down, so I took an A13 Cruiser Tank and arrived in the centre of the town at about 21.00 hours.'

A9 had shed a track and so Corporal Stuart was left behind to effect repairs and he managed it '...by using No 9 punches out of the MG kit, having no track pins.'

Major Reeves in his requisitioned A13 and several other tank commanders drove on towards the harbour area to find fuel and a place to carry out essential repairs. They parked '...in a rather disorganized body lining two sides of a road near the docks', and he recalled the atmosphere which greeted the tank crews as they entered Calais.

'It was just getting dark and a most eerie feeling pervaded the city which was then deserted. It was a beautiful night, no wind and a rising full moon, but despite this there was an atmosphere of intense excitement and the very silence was far more foreboding than the noise of battle. That we were surrounded was certain. It does not take much imagination to appreciate what the situation was like in Calais that night. Information of enemy movements was scanty to say the least of it. We had seen large German armoured columns approaching the city from the Coquelles ridge. We did not know what the defences (if any) were like or where they were. Consequently we were expecting German tanks to enter at any minute and from any direction. It was not a pleasant situation...Nobody seemed to know where our lorries were, and with the exception of hard rations, the troops had had nothing to eat or drink since the landing in France the day before. The general morale would have risen enormously if a hot brew of tea could have been served out.'

At around 11pm Brigadier Nicholson again met Colonel Keller at the Pont St Pierre. They discussed the issue of support in order to clear the road to Gravelines. Keller was then able to relay the outcome of the discussion and the following information to his squadron commanders, 'Calais is surrounded. Heavy bombing is expected tonight and a powerful attack will probably be put in in the morning.' It was the final confirmation, if any were needed, of the worst fears of some of his senior officers.

The 23 May had been a long day too for Lieuteant Airey Neave. During the evening he had marched north from his defensive positions in Coulogne where he and his troop of 2 Battery of 1 Searchlight Regiment had been in action earlier against other elements of 1 Panzer Division at approximately the same time as 3RTR had been fighting their battle near

Hames Boucres. He and his men had done their best but they had not been able to hold the Germans back indefinitely. Any illusions of a non-fighting role had been dashed earlier in the day and Neave was by now well aware that he and the surviving members of his regiment would have to fight it out like the rest of the Calais garrison. He was not, however, aware of the fact that British tanks had been landed in Calais. As Neave approached the Hôtel de Ville at 9 pm he heard the rattling of tank tracks amid the gathering gloom and shadows of the Parc St. Pierre. He wondered whether the Germans had succeeded in overtaking him and were even now working their way through the streets of the town.

A PzKmpf Mk III works its way through ruined dwellings.

CHAPTER SEVEN

THIS LITTLE ACTION

With Colonel Goldney's order to concentrate at their Troop HQ's at dawn on 23 May the men of 1 Searchlight Regiment had packed up their equipment and had left their isolated positions in the fields beyond the boundaries of Calais to receive their orders. Lieutenant Airey Neave had directed his sixty or seventy men of 'F' Troop to dig trenches and strengthen the road-blocks to the south and south-east of Coulogne out along the straight road leading to Pont de Briques. A little way beyond the Pont de Briques lay 'G' Troop HQ at a house on the canal side and a little further still, over the canal and the level crossing beyond, lay Ferme de Vendroux, HQ of 'C' Troop of 1 Searchlight battery under 2/Lieutenant R J Barr. During the day the ranks of the Searchlights were stiffened with the addition of two officers and 168 men of 2 Searchlight Regiment who had been stationed near Boulogne. They were divided up between the two batteries of 1 Searchlight Regiment.

**Lieutenant Colonel
R M Goldney**

As the men dug in, built up their barriers and sited their handful of Bren guns and Boys anti-tank rifles, the forward units of Assault Group Kruger of 1 Panzer Division were preparing to wheel east, towards the Aa Canal and Dunkirk. Their line of advance would take them towards Guines and their eventual encounter with 3RTR near Hames Boucres. Even though 1 Panzer was reduced in strength due to fatigue and mechanical and battle damage to vehicles and equipment it was nevertheless a formidable 'Goliath' compared to the 'David' of the territorials of the Searchlights. In any case, Guderian wanted to conserve his troops and machines of 1 Panzer Division for the drive to Dunkirk. He was keen to avoid a major battle at this stage, opting instead to by-pass Calais to the south and east, leaving the town to Schall's 10 Panzer Division. If, however, the advance went smoothly and Kruger encountered little opposition as he pushed eastward, he was given sufficient leeway to allow the infantry regiment on his left to detach from the main thrust of the division, cross the Marck Canal and take Calais 'by surprise' from the east. Had Guderian known the extent of the defences and the firepower of the scattered platoons and detachments of 1QVR and 1 Searchlight Regiment during the night of 22/23 of May history may well have recorded the fall of Calais several days before it was finally taken. As it was, Guderian's mind was on Dunkirk. Calais, if it could be taken with little effort, would be a bonus. Barring his way, and ready to make Guderian and Kruger fight for every inch of ground, lay the tanks and the 'terriers' of the British Army.

It was around 12.30 pm when a dispatch rider roared into the farmyard of Ferme de Vendroux with the news that three German light tanks were heading towards Les Attaques from the direction of Guines. This was more than two hours before the battle with 3RTR near Hames Boucres, proving that Kruger's forces had already passed in front of Colonel Keller's intended line of advance towards St. Omer well before Keller had set out. The village of Les Attaques lay 7 kilometres south-west of Calais along the main road to St. Omer and the capture of the bridge across the Canal de Calais, St. Omer and the cross roads in the village were vital to the German advance. The seizure of the bridge and the cross roads offered Kruger a route which would not take him too far north and risk contacting Allied troops in the southern outskirts of Calais or too far south to become bogged down among the many dykes and ditches which criss-crossed the low-lying land around Ardres.

Second Lieutenant Barr headed for Les Attaques with three detachments of 'C' Troop. When he arrived he determined to hold the bridge and the crossroads and started to build a road-block on the Calais side of the intersection. An abandoned lorry was pressed into service and was driven into a position in the centre of the cross-roads while a bus was parked in the middle of the side road which led towards the bridge and then to Guines, in the hope that there would be insufficient space for a tank to pass through. As a further precaution, three more detachments were sent to block the crossroads at le Colombier, two and a half kilometres back along the main road and a little over one kilometre south-west of Colonel Goldney's HQ at Orphanage Farm. When they had done what they could, they waited.

At around two o'clock Barr's men looked out from their positions on the east bank of the canal to see three German light tanks approaching the bridge from the direction of Guines. Barr's men opened fire with their Bren guns, rifles and anti-tank rifles but could not prevent the tanks from crossing the bridge and gaining a toehold on the eastern bank.They succeeded in preventing the light tanks from making further headway but by now medium tanks had advanced in support of their advance guard and the fire from their 2cm guns was making the Searchlights' position untenable. Barr ordered a gradual withdrawal towards the houses beyond the crossroads as the German tanks attempted to break out of the 'bottleneck' of the side street leading from the bridge and enter the main Calais - St. Omer road. This was a crucial phase of the action. If the German

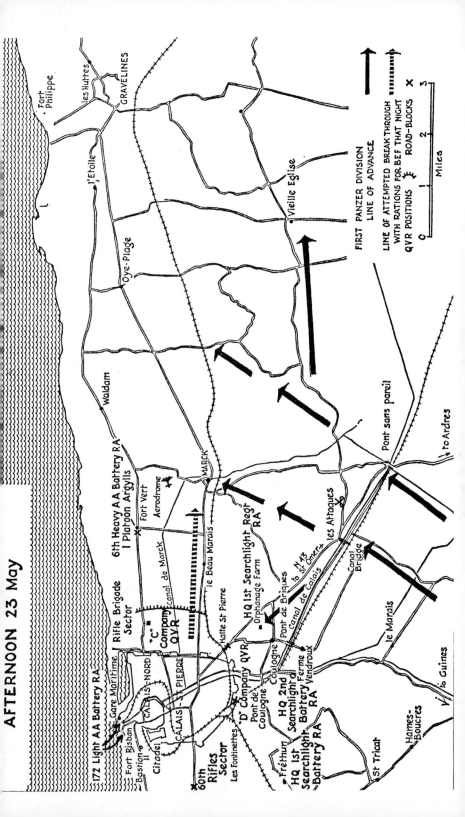

AFTERNOON 23 May

FIRST PANZER DIVISION
LINE OF ADVANCE

LINE OF ATTEMPTED BREAK-THROUGH
WITH RATIONS FOR BEF THAT NIGHT
QVR POSITIONS   ROAD-BLOCKS   X

0   1   2   3
Miles

Fort
Philippe

les Huttes

GRAVELINES

l'Etoile

Oye-Plage

Vieille Eglise

Waldam

Pont sans pareil

to Ardres

MARCK

Fort Vert
Aerodrome

6th Heavy AA Battery RA
I Platoon Argylls

Rifle Brigade
Sector

"C"
Company
QVR

Canal de Marck

le Beau Marais

Halte St Pierre

HQ 1st Searchlight Regt
RA

les Attaques

172 Light AA Battery RA

Gare Maritime

Fort Risban
Bastion II
Citadel

CALAIS—NORD

CALAIS—ST PIERRE

Les Fontinettes

60th

Rifles
Sector

"D" Company QVR

Pont de
Coulogne

Coulogne

Pont de Briques

Canal de Calais

to St Omer

N43

Orphanage Farm

Canal Bridge

le Marais

to Guines

Fréthun

HQ 2nd
Searchlight
Battery
RA

HQ 1st
Searchlight
Battery RA

Ferme
Vendroux

St Tricat

Hames-
Boucres

tanks negotiated the crossroads they would be free to fan out and rampage in all directions with the encirclement of the Searchlights the likely outcome. They re-doubled their efforts and every time a light tank nosed its way onto the main Calais-St Omer road it was driven back. This scene was replayed five times until the medium tanks found the range of the houses concealing Barr's men and forced them out with accurate shellfire.

At this point the Germans altered their tactics. A medium tank drove up the side street pushing the empty bus before it all the way up to the crossroads, where it was used as a battering ram to sweep the lorry away as well. This was the breakthrough the Germans had worked for. Two more medium tanks, following in the wake of the first, drove up and passed straight over the crossroads taking the road which led into the rest of Les Attaques and which eventually came back on itself and re-entered the main road a little over half a kilometre to the north and in rear of the Searchlights road block. A third medium tank turned north towards Calais and threatened the road block. Behind them, like bees swarming from a hive, came light tanks in support. Barr had already sent for reinforcements from 2 Searchlight Battery at the Pont de Coulogne and some of the men had answered his call with an eager enthusiasm which betrayed their lack of military experience. Returning to Pont de Coulogne from a visit to Calais,

German mortar team in action in the suburbs of Calais.

Battery Quartermaster Sergeant W R Kinnear found that the ammunition lorry had vanished along with some of the men. He was told that it had been driven out to intercept an 'enemy tank'. Kinnear jumped into his Austin Seven and drove out through Coulogne down the main road towards Les Attaques. He arrived just in time to see the ammunition lorry explode under fire from a German flame thrower. Thankfully most of the occupants managed to get out in time and escaped towards Calais.

By now the time was approaching 5pm and Barr's 'C' Troop had been holding Les Attaques for almost three hours. As the minutes ticked by and the German tanks worked their way around the Searchlights' positions it became clear that the small force was all but surrounded. By 5 o'clock Barr was forced to surrender.

Meanwhile, on the southern outskirts of Coulogne, three kilometres to the north-west along the canal, attempts by German infantry to advance to the west of the Calais-St. Omer road had been checked by men of Lieutenant Airey Neave's 'F' Troop, HQ troops from 1 Searchlight Regiment and the HQ staff of 172 Light AA Battery. Neave's men were in their trenches and at their blocks in Coulogne but the rest had taken up position on the rising ground a little way south of Colonel Goldney's HQ at Orphanage Farm.

Even as the first of the German light tanks had probed the bridge at Les Attaques at two o'clock that afternoon, Kruger's infantry had advanced on their left and had captured a stationary hospital train waiting for the all clear to enter Calais. At Orphanage Farm Goldney was preparing to defend his position with the help of the padre, the medical officer and a few men. He had sent the rest of his HQ staff out on patrol under the command of Lieutenant Duncan Nash, to move forward and secure an advanced position on the rising ground less then one kilometre south of the farm. To Nash's left was a French anti-tank gun at a large house beside the Calais-St.Omer road and to his right were the HQ staff of 172 Light AA Battery. A little after 2pm the German infantry attacked the British positions from some empty railway trucks. The British on the high ground replied as did Neave's men from their trenches in Coulogne, a little way to the west.

Duncan Nash

> 'I had posted Bren gunners at the south-east corner of the village but they could not see over the ridge. The Germans now opened up with very heavy rifle and automatic fire to which we replied. Unfortunately, my Bren gunners, not being able to see the Germans, fired over the ridge narrowly missing Colonel Goldney's staff. A dispatch rider roared over the fields from Orphanage Farm with a well deserved "rocket" from the Colonel and the Brens were moved forward.'

As Neave ordered his guns forward the Germans brought up heavier and more destructive weapons. Terrified refugees were still trying to get

81

through the British barricades and make their escape into Calais. Lieutenant Neave had stopped one such group, a family of Austrian Jews, at his barricade and as they pleaded with him to let them pass there was a deafening crash.

'A mortar bomb burst on the roof of the Mairie, showering us with broken tiles and twigs. The village was accurately bombed for fifteen minutes, paving stones were hurled into the air and several houses caught fire. When the barrage lifted, I walked along the main street. A young girl lay dead at the corner of the road. A soldier gently pulled her tartan skirt over her knees.

At approximately the same time as Barr was forced to surrender at Les Attaques, some of the German tanks which had continued their push towards Coulogne were pressing the left flank of Nash's party of Searchlights and the HQ of 172 Light AA Battery on the slightly higher ground to the east of the canal. They held on to their isolated position until the fire from the tanks forced them to withdraw and rejoin Goldney at Orphanage Farm. Coulogne and Orphanage Farm had now been held for three hours as had Les Attaques and the resistance had already proved to be a considerable thorn in the left flank of Kruger's Assault Group. The Germans next brought up field guns in an attempt to resolve the situation and for over an hour Orphanage Farm was shelled mercilessly. From Coulogne, 800 metres away, Neave could see the shells bursting amongst the trees surrounding the farm. By 7pm Goldney had decided that he could no longer defend his position and he ordered a withdrawal in small parties, first to the road block held by 13 platoon of 'D' Company 1 QVR at the Halte St. Pierre, two kilometres back down the road towards Calais, and thence to the ramparts. As they evacuated the buildings Orphanage Farm was set alight by shell-fire.

Neave's last job was to blow up the 'Cuckoo', the code name for the experimental sound location equipment which the Searchlights had begun to use before he made good his escape towards Calais. Later that evening he would hear the jangling of the tank tracks of 3RTR near the Parc St. Pierre as they too returned from their fight with 1 Panzer Division.

As darkness fell it had become clear to the Germans that a surprise attack and an easy victory at Calais was out of the question. The War Diary of 1 Panzer Division, stated that at nightfall Assault Group Kruger 'stood at the gates of Calais', but that it was 'strongly held by the enemy and that a surprise attack was out of the question.' The tank action at Hames Boucres and the dogged resistance of the Searchlights at Les Attaques, Orphanage Farm and Coulogne had given Guderian food for thought. If Calais had fallen that day 10 Panzer Division may have been used in the advance on Dunkirk. One can only speculate as to what may have happened in such a case. What happened in fact was that the engagements

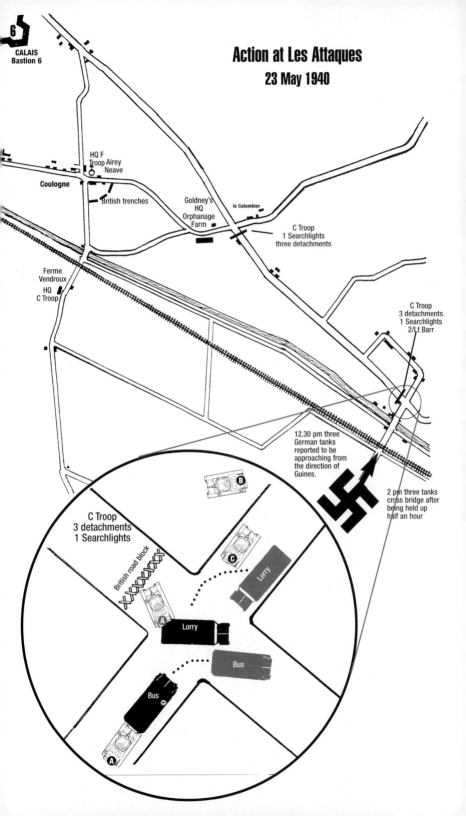

Action at Les Attaques
23 May 1940

6
CALAIS
Bastion 6

HQ F
Troop Airey
Neave

Coulogne

British trenches

Goldney's
HQ
Orphanage
Farm

le Colombier

C Troop
1 Searchlights
three detachments

Ferme
Vendroux

HQ
C Troop

C Troop
3 detachments
1 Searchlights
2/Lt Barr

12.30 pm three
German tanks
reported to be
approaching from
the direction of
Guines.

2 pm three tanks
cross bridge after
being held up
half an hour

C Troop
3 detachments
1 Searchlights

British road block

Lorry

Lorry

Bus

Bus

B

C

A

A

Brigadier Nicholson

on that day succeeded in giving 1 Panzer Division a 'bloody nose' and that if the resistance shown in the battles of 23 May was to be repeated by the troops still to be engaged in Calais itself then the coming battle would be anything but a pushover. That the majority of those troops had so recently arrived that very afternoon, Guderian could not know. The two regular battalions of 30 Brigade were given a breathing space, albeit a short-lived one, in which to begin to get organized due to the actions of the troops of 3RTR and 1 Searchlight Regiment.

Later, commenting on the defence of Les Attaques and Orphanage Farm whilst compiling his unfinished report on the battle of Calais in a prisoner of war camp, Brigadier Nicholson wrote, *'This little action succeeded in delaying the advance of an enemy armoured column by this route by some five hours.'* As Guderian ordered 1 Panzer Division to push on towards Gravelines and Dunkirk that evening, it was left to General Schall's 10 Panzer Division to break the heart of Calais.

The face of exhaustion. A German motorcyclist rests with his rifle ready to use in an instant.

CHAPTER EIGHT

AN EXTREMELY NERVE WRACKING BUSINESS

Whilst the battles of the afternoon had been taking place the unloading of the vehicles for the Green Jackets had begun. The saga of the unloading of the motor transport ships, the *Kohistan* carrying the vehicles of 2KRRC and the *Canterbury* carrying those of 1RB, ultimately led to the destruction or loss of at least half of 1RB's transport and vital equipment which put it at a disadvantage during the battle. It went on all through the night interrupted by air raids and German shelling. The British stevedores were exhausted having unloaded the 350,000 rations intended for the rest of the BEF converging on Dunkirk on to the dockside the previous day. The French took no risks during the bombardments and consequently work stopped for several hours during the night. The unloading of the *Kohistan* was not completed until 4.30 am on 24 May when wounded from one hospital train began to be carried aboard, but at that time half the RB transport was still on board the *Canterbury*.

To add to the confusion, throughout the night of the 23/24, it was unclear whether 30 Brigade would be evacuated, as indeed were around 2000 of 20 Guards Brigade from Boulogne on the morning of 24 May. At three am a message was sent to Nicholson to the effect that the evacuation of 30 Brigade had been decided, 'in principle', presumably in line with War Office thinking regarding the evacuation of the Boulogne garrison. He received that message on the Dunkirk road whilst he was overseeing preparations to get the rations convoy to Dunkirk underway. By 7.30 am the plan to evacuate was becoming known amongst the troops and what happened to Rifleman Roy Archer during unloading may have been a direct result of the apparent confusion abroad at the time. As a wireless 'pick up' driver Roy Archer had remained in the harbour all night to assist with the unloading of the RB transport.

'We arrived and went alongside the quay near the Gare Maritime. There was a "stonk" of German shells landing in the harbour nearby and the French stevedores, who were unloading the ships, ran off leaving the cranes unmanned and out of commission. Some men of a searchlight detachment and our men got the cranes in action and the unloading began again. First the deck cargo of trucks and four gallon cans of petrol had to be got off before the holds could be opened up for the vehicles to be landed. As the trucks' petrol tanks were empty, they had to be man-handled to a bit of spare ground, where we were told to put our vehicles out of action by Captain Peel. I expect that he felt the Germans would sweep in and capture all the

equipment. What a shambles! I had to smash the engine block and the wireless. I did manage to salvage the 'Elgin' watch, a highly accurate watch mounted in a wireless truck for timing signals. A hospital train steamed slowly into the Gare Maritime and started to unload its cargo of severely wounded. All the dead were laid in rows and covered with blankets. The train had been three days being shunted about escaping from German troops. The padre, Rev Wingfield -Digby, worked like a Trojan tending the wounded.'

No one is quite clear who gave the order for what happened next but at 7.30 am the Sea Transport Officer at the Gare Maritime halted the unloading of the *Canterbury* and ordered the holds to be closed saying that he had received permission from Brigadier Nicholson. Wounded from the second hospital train were carried aboard by Rifle Brigade men and the ship sailed for England at 8.30 am., taking with it half of 1RB's vehicles and equipment. It was followed at noon by the *Kohistan*, the last ship to leave Calais before the order came to fight it out to the end.

Well before the ships sailed, however, riflemen of 1RB and tanks of 3RTR had been in action during the night. During the evening the Bren carriers of 'A' Company's scout platoon under 2/Lieutenant Tony Rolt set out to patrol the Gravelines road towards Dunkirk in advance of the rations column. They reached Fort Vert as darkness fell and gathered from the locals that German tanks were already in the area. These were tanks of 1 Panzer Division which had by now encircled Calais after their engagement with 3RTR earlier in the day. Although a DR brought verbal orders from Captain Peter Peel temporarily in charge of 'A' Company, to withdraw, Rolt asked for written confirmation, such were the fears of false reports spread by 'Fifth Columnists'. In the meantime he placed his vehicles in 'all round defence' positions for the night and waited for the rations column to pass. It never did. As darkness fell Rolt found himself surrounded by the bonfires of the tanks at the spearhead of 1 Panzer Division which Rifleman Sandford could see from his vantage point on the eastern ramparts near the Pont de Gravelines. It was only after he received confirmation of his orders to withdraw early next morning that Rolt somehow extricated himself from the German noose and returned to 1RB positions without loss.

Whilst Rolt had been spending the night watching the bonfires of 1 Panzer Division glowing all around him on either side of the Calais-Gravelines road, another patrol had come into contact with the German tanks but this time they had managed to push straight through to Gravelines itself.

Brigadier Nicholson had met with Lieutenant Colonel Keller at 11.00 pm at the Pont St. Pierre and had asked him to send a patrol towards Marck. It consisted of Major Reeves in his A13 cruiser and three light tanks

NCOs of a panzer unit check their position during the drive to the north west. The armoured car is a Sd Kfz 232, eight wheel drive with a crew of four.

of 'B' Squadron. They were to check if the road was held and to return to Calais if the opposition was too strong. If not they were to get through to Gravelines and contact 69 Brigade already there. Major Reeves thought it a 'ticklish' job to do in the dark but it was a moonlit night and his tanks set off with Sergeant Jim Cornwell commanding the point tank followed by Peter Williams the troop commander and then the reserve light tank. Major Reeves followed ready to give covering fire with his 2-pounder gun. Nothing happened for the first two miles as they drove out of Calais but their spirits dropped when they saw an ominous looking black mass in the middle of the road. It was a road -block consisting of old lorries leaving only just enough room to get through. Reeves pushed on and quickly realized that whatever happened there was no turning back as the murky outlines of tanks and men in large numbers could be made out on either side of the road.

'We pushed on rapidly and in another few hundred yards we were among German troops who were sitting and walking about on either side of the road. They did not seem to be in the least perturbed at seeing us, and I soon realized that they thought we were their own tanks... Some of the

German troops waved to us as we passed and we returned the compliment. If we had fired a shot our number would have been up as they could have trapped us between any two of the numerous road blocks which we passed safely through. Peter Williams stopped his tank on one occasion thinking the soldiers were French and said "Parlez -vous Anglais?" The German merely shook his head and walked off. After we had been travelling through Germans for about two miles, they appeared to be getting suspicious and one or two dispatch riders came up and switched torches on my tank and moved off rapidly as if to report. No-one fired at us. I tried in vain to get a wireless message through to the Battalion, but the wireless was not working that night and no warning or information could be sent back. At length we arrived at Marck where there is a bridge over the canal. It was here that Sergeant Cornwell reported that there were eight tank mines on the bridge. These were connected by a strip of metal across the top so that if a tank ran over one, the whole lot would go off.'

Sergeant Cornwell in the point tank tried to fire at them with his machine gun but to no avail. He then asked for assistance.

'I called up Bill Reeves and he used his 2-pounder but no luck. The noise we made roused the enemy and things were getting a bit hectic so I asked him to give me covering fire while I had a look. Sure enough they were mines about six of them joined by a metal strip. Luckily the tow rope on the front of the tank was handy and I got Davis (the driver) to come up close and I hooked the rope over the metal.'

Major Reeves could only watch as Jim Cornwell got out of his tank to remove the mines.

*'This was **an extremely nerve wracking business**, especially as we had seen two Germans on the other side of the bridge who had temporarily disappeared owing to our firing. There was dead silence as the Sergeant quietly crept from his tank, revolver in hand and proceeded to attach the tow rope of his tank to the mines. It was an eerie business and the bright moonlight seemed to accentuate the feeling of hidden danger that must have been surrounding us. We felt every second counted as it was only a matter of time before the Germans could bring terrific odds to bear against us. At last the mines were removed. It was only a matter of minutes but it seemed like hours.'*

Having crossed the bridge their troubles were not over. They ran into coils of barbed wire which wrapped themselves round the sprockets of the tanks and brought two to a standstill. It took another twenty minutes to cut it away with wire cutters. After the bridge they met no further opposition and had a clear run through to Gravelines, which they reached at 2am on 24 May. It had been an extraordinary journey which had concluded successfully due to cool thinking under pressure, courage and a great deal of luck. Major Reeves' Troop fought in Gravelines the next day, knocking out five German tanks and two troop carriers.

Meanwhile as 1RB vehicles had become available they had been sent to Major Boy Hamilton-Russell who eventually received four composite platoons made up of riflemen from all companies. Five tanks of 'C' Squadron 3RTR under Major F V Lyons were to lead the convoy followed by three Bren carriers then three platoons in trucks. Another two platoons under Captain Michael Smiley, Hamilton Russell's second in command, were to act as rearguard. 1RB were on the starting line on the outskirts of Calais at midnight and there they awaited the tanks. 3RTR had had a hard day already, but every minute they waited diminished their chances of success.

The tanks finally arrived and the convoy snaked past the Dunkirk Gate

Motorcyclists of Guderian's Korps resting by the roadside. A six-wheeled heavy armoured car (Sd Kfz 231) is passing.

in half light between 4 and 5 am watched by Brigadier Nicholson himself. They did not get far. Running into the same road blocks at le Beau Marais as Major Reeves had done earlier, the far larger rations convoy had none of his luck. The tanks halted and a dismounted attack was put in by 1RB.

Doug Wheeler was part of the convoy.

> *'I was sent to join a convoy made up mostly of men from 'B' Company which was building up on the other side of the canal. I sat on my bike all night awake waiting for the convoy to start and at first light we crept out of town down a long, quite wide, straight road into the sun, we were obviously going east towards Dunkirk. We halted some miles out of town under heavy shell and mortar fire at the head of the convoy from the south of the road. The 15cwt truck in front of me was hit by a mortar bomb and a large piece of metal hit the Bren carrier behind me. This would be about nine or ten in the morning. An old friend of mine from the depot days Sergeant Lane was hit in the legs pretty badly and I helped him to get into a ditch under cover. He gave me his rifle and bandolier of ammunition and told me to take up "all round defence" positions, one of the basic rules when a convoy stopped. I did this and got up on the roof of a small house, loaded the rifle and looked for the enemy.'*

Rifleman Wheeler was called down by an NCO who felt he had left his motorcycle and was jeopardizing the position, but he was immediately taken away by an officer who gathered some men together in a hedgerow as shells and bullets flew up and down the road. The officer told Wheeler to ride back to Calais, find the CO and report that the convoy was returning.

When the convoy had come under fire Major Hamilton-Russell had tried to get his men around the flanks of the Germans but had found it impossible to break through under heavy and accurate mortar fire. 2/Lieutenant Edward Bird's platoon particularly ran into very heavy opposition to the south of the road and lost touch with the rest of the convoy. Back in Calais Brigadier Nicholson and Lieutenant Colonel Chandos Hoskyns waited anxiously for news. Reports confirmed that the convoy was about to be surrounded and Hamilton-Russell withdrew his men at around 10.30 am. They arrived back in Calais at 11.00 am, where the remaining platoons of 'B' Company were split up to form road blocks or patrols or to reinforce other companies. Two men were killed, including L/Corporal Cross, and several others were wounded.

Any possibility of breaking through to the east had vanished with the failure of the convoy and Brigadier Nicholson could now give his full attention to the defence of the outer perimeter. It was just as well that he could. By the time Hamilton-Russell's force had arrived back in Calais the defence of the outer perimeter to the west and south-west had been raging for six hours.

CHAPTER NINE

NOW WE KNOW, THE ENGLISHMAN DEFENDS CALAIS

At dawn on Friday 24 May a rain of heavy mortar shells on the QVR positions of 'D' Company to the south and west of the outer perimeter signalled the onset of 10 Panzer Division's attack as the vanguard of the German 69 Rifle Regiment moved north after capturing Guines. It was to be a day of fierce fighting. The Germans pushed hardest against the QVR platoons blocking the roads to Fréthun, Coulogne and Ardres. At 11 platoon's road block near the hump backed bridge on the Fréthun road, Rifleman Sam Kydd was watching.

'After about an hour of peering and ...and wondering and waiting – it happened. A German tank lumbered slowly and ominously into view and stopped about 200 yards away. Some trigger-happy machine gunner opened up on his own account and all hell was let loose. The section I was in deployed to the right to approach at an angle to engage it with our Boys Anti-Tank Gun... as we crouched and edged forward...we were met with a heavy burst of machine gun fire. The section scattered leaving two dead and retreated hastily to the main party at the roadblock where the rest of them were heavily engaged firing at German soldiers advancing behind the tank. The **Rifleman Sam Kydd** *air was filled with whining shells and bullets and it was obviously impossible to hold such a force so we disengaged...We retired to a ridge of high round... a place like the banks of a disused reservoir which commanded a view of the road we had just left.'*

11 platoon had been ordered to withdraw at 7 am to the line of the ramparts from Bastion 6 westward to Bastion 9 which was held by platoons of 'A' and 'D' Companies 2KRRC, along with 2/Lieutenant Brewester's 12 platoon which had held the block at the crossroads of the route de Coulogne and the Chemin de Grand Voyeau. Brewester now withdrew to a position on the right of the iron railway bridge over the Canal de Calais, the Pont de Fer. 13 platoon which had been positioned at the Halte St. Pierre had already withdrawn to the ramparts. These platoons along with around 60 Searchlights personnel, now plugged gaps in the extended 2KRRC front on the southern face of the outer perimeter. The Germans

Lage der 10. Pz. Div. am 24.5.40. 8⁰⁰

10. Schtz. Brig.
S.R. 86
I./S.R. 69
1./A.R. 90
1. Kp. Pi. 49
1. Kp. Pz. Jg. L-A
1. Battr. Fla 71

S.R. 69 (o I)
I./A.R. 90 (o 1)
1. Kp. Pi 49
1 Battr. Fla 71
1. Kp. Pz. Jg. L-A

Franzosen
170 Offz. – 2000
450 Mann

Marsch der 10. Pz. Div. vom 23./24.5.

S.R. 86
I./S.R. 86
1./A.R. 90
Pz. Jg. 251

Div. Stab
Stab 10. Schtz. Brig.
S.R. 69
I./S.R. 86
A.R. 90 m. I./A.R. 105
Pz. Jg. Lehr-Abt.
Pi-Btn. 49
Flak-Abt. 71
4. Pz. Brig.

continued to press their attacks against the ramparts all morning with heavy machine-gun and mortar fire and for a time 12 platoon, with the railway embankment directly behind it, was completely pinned down. As the hours wore on and the fighting intensified the casualties mounted. Towards noon single rifle shots from houses in the Boulevard Curie behind them signalled that the line had been breached in places by small parties of the German 69 Rifle Regiment.

Further west the German 86 Rifle Regiment had mopped up any resistance on their advance from Marquise and had occupied Coquelles during the night. They had soon been joined by the first batteries of medium artillery which took up positions near the wooden windmill on top of the ridge above the village. Hubert Borchert, a front line photographer, was with them.

> 'On the last hill we stop and wait for the dawn. Before us, in the yielding foggy dust of dawn we perceive the sea. We are all joyfully excited and moved, from the commander of the Rifle Brigade to the private soldier. Now we know: the assault of the Schnellen Truppen has succeeded. We are standing only some kilometres from the Channel. This moment at Calais, as if emerging from the sea, red like blood, the sun rises. The many roofs, gables and towers, the old lighthouse and the rows of cranes seem to be silhouettes. The Town Hall's tower tops them all. From the west and south the brigade attacks at dawn. Platoons of the reconniassance battalion and of the motorcycle company, combat groups reinforced by heavy MG's and heavy trench-mortars, advance. The target is the railway line which, in the west runs like a fortification line along the whole town, and the Fort Nieulay. It is to be taken by a surprise raid.'

The German gunners now began to fire at their targets. On the western face of the outer perimeter 'B' and 'C' Companies of 2KRRC were subjected to constant shell fire from just after dawn which developed during the morning and went on well into the evening, as the German batteries plastered the line of the railway, especially around the Pont Jourdan where the boulevard Léon Gambetta crossed the railway track. 'B' Company HQ was in buildings between the railway bridge and the canal.

Second Lieutenant Davies-Scourfield's 5 platoon had been given the task of defending,

> '...a high semi-circular fortification, marked on the map as Bastion 9 but which has always remained in my memory as 'The Redoubt': it had concrete blocks along it at intervals, with plenty of cover from scrubby bushes...Digging was fairly easy, and if we had had some mines and wire, some artillery to provide defensive fire and a weapon with some chance of destroying a German medium tank, then the Redoubt could have become a formidable strongpoint. It lay immediately on the left of the main road to the village of Coquelles... and overlooked all approaches from that direction...'

Left: Original map of 10th Panzer Division showing the positions of its units at 8.00 am on 24 May. BUNDESARCHIV FREIBURG

The attack on the defenders' positions began with an artillery barrage.
TAYLOR LIBRARY

After the men had dug in they waited. Sergeant Henry Wall, a well respected and level headed NCO turned to Corporal Ron Savage and said, 'You know Ron, we'll be lucky to get out of this.' The words were spoken without a hint of fear or drama. It was only on reflection in later years that Ron Savage realized that the experienced men probably knew instinctively what they were up against.

A few shells fell on Bastion 9 during the first hour of daylight and it was clear the German gunners had marked the defences. The German plan was to push infantry forward, either side of Fort Nieulay to threaten the 2KRRC line on the western defences. In order to do that they would have to silence the British anti-aircraft guns near the coast at Oyez Farm and the French naval guns at Fort Lapin. They would also have to crush the defenders of the ruined fort which they could see below them. The battle for Fort Nieulay was on.

The origins of the strategic importance of Fort Nieulay as an advanced defensive position for the town of Calais could be traced back hundreds of years. A defensive position had stood on or near the site for centuries and the fort had been completely rebuilt by Vauban between 1677 and 1680 but by 1939 it had been abandoned and sold by the French military and an air of decay had descended upon it. The gates of the two main entrances, the Porte Dauphine to the west and the Porte Royale to the east had fallen from their hinges and the buildings were falling down. It was to this fort, almost a ruin and deprived of any military value, that a small force of British troops came on the evening of 23 May 1940, to join a small French garrison in helping to stem the advance of an entire Panzer Division.

Captain Tim Munby, in command of the scout platoon of the 1QVR, had landed in Calais on the afternoon of Wednesday 22 May. On 23 May at 11.15 am, Captain Munby was ordered to take his scout platoon and block the road to Boulogne which had been left uncovered by the move of 3RTR south towards Guines. He had first chosen a site a little way along the road from Bastion 9 but had then moved forward to a site 150 yards in advance of the south gate of Fort Nieulay, well beyond the line of the old ramparts. He had improvised his block by noon using a lorry and farm implements scrounged from nearby fields and yards. At 3 pm 2/Lieutenant Freddy Nelson, commanding 6 platoon of 'B' Company 1QVR, in position at Oyez Farm on the coast road to Sangatte, moved across country to relieve him but as there was no transport available to take Captain Munby back towards Calais, both platoons remained at the road block. Rifleman Edward Lyme had been with Nelson at Oyez Farm and had spent the night in a ditch as Number Two on a Bren gun with his pal Tom Shewring. When his platoon had been ordered elsewhere he had no idea where they were going except that it seemed '...vaguely further back towards Calais across fields.' Orders had been issued that no civilian refugees or unarmed Allied troops were to enter the town and Captain Munby's force had been turning them back all afternoon. Captain Munby wrote,

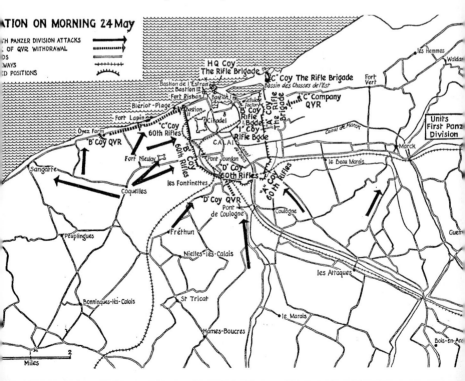

'The Germans were reported to be only ten miles away and it was a heartrending business to have to turn back carloads of refugees, mostly old men, women and children, virtually into the arms of the enemy. Several French motor battalions fell back through us in pretty good order, but for the most part our Allies presented a pretty sorry spectacle. Many Belgian battalions had been on the road for a long time, as the German breakthrough had occurred before they were mobilized; ordered to rally in succession at Boulogne and Gravelines, it was not surprising they were losing heart, many of them having marched 150 miles.' PRO WO217/4

They had not been there long when a lone German dispatch rider rode straight up to the block and was taken prisoner. He had somehow overshot his own front line. His captivity would not last long, however. Captain Munby could see a road block formed by a detachment of the 229th Anti-Tank Battery RA with one 2-pounder anti-tank gun covering the road some 500 metres behind him but he was uneasy about his position. The road was straight, the ground was flat and intersected by ditches and his men had no tools for digging in. His meagre road block would not hold a tank attack for long. At 4.15 pm, after a visit from Lieutenant Colonel Ellison-MacCartney, Captain Munby disappeared from his position much to the surprise of his men. He had decided to approach Capitaine Herremann, commanding the French detachment inside Fort Nieulay, with a view to moving his men into the fort. Herreman was not enthusiastic but Munby was insistent and pointed out the weaknesses in his present position. Herreman telephoned his superiors and at last agreed to let Munby's force in on condition that they acted under French orders and that they, '...should not retire from the Fort having once entered it.' Munby agreed and by 9 pm his men were inside. Corporal John Dexter was with Captain Munby.

'We were on the roadside and Captain Munby had difficulty in convincing the French commander... that we should share with them what little cover they had in the tumbled ruins of the ancient Fort Nieulay.The French had assumed we had arrived there only to retreat.'

Munby found that Capitaine Herreman was in command of a mixed force consisting of a Lieutenant and forty other ranks as well as a Lieutenant of Marines and six marines armed with a 25 mm anti-tank gun, two 13.2 mm, heavy Hotchkiss machine guns and forty rifles. Munby's force had six Bren guns, one anti-tank rifle and twenty-five rifles. Munby surveyed the scene. The area of the fort covered about five acres and its walls were thirty to forty feet high.

'In the centre was a ruined keep; shelters were provided by old tunnels and shelters at the foot of the walls. The gate was a flimsy affair of modern iron palings and on the east side was an old building, renovated to some extent to provide kitchens and officers' quarters. There was no water supply, nor any sanitary arrangements. At three corners were large bastions.'

Fort Nieulay.   **Site of farm house used by German sniper, 24 May**

The ruinous condition meant that it was a less than perfect site to defend, but it was far better than taking cover behind a lorry and a few ploughs on a straight, level road.

As the French were holding the south-west bastion, Munby deployed the British force in the north-west and north-east bastions. 6 platoon of 'B' Company and 2 scout section took the north-west corner where Munby also established his HQ. 1 scout section took the north-east bastion whilst 3 scout section took the one anti-tank rifle and joined the party of six French marines with their 25 mm anti-tank gun behind a lorry blocking the Dauphine Gate and covering the road to Coquelles.

There were various 'alarums and excursions' during the early hours of 24 May. At 3 am the men who were not on guard duty were woken by gunfire at the main gate. French sentries had opened fire on three men of the Searchlights who were trying to get in. Munby persuaded the French that there was nothing amiss and they were allowed to enter. Half an hour later the force were ordered to stand to on the ancient walls and saw three Very lights arc ominously into the sky away in the direction of Coquelles. A little over an hour later the Nieulay garrison watched as three scout carriers of 'B' Company 2KRRC under 2/Lieutenant Dick Scott drove past the fort in the direction of Coquelles on the first of his patrols which had been ordered by Major Jack Poole, and returned almost immediately carrying some 20 Searchlights personnel who had been stranded during the withdrawal into Calais. They had been rescued by Scott's party from under the noses of the advancing Germans and were taken back towards the KRRC positions near Bastion 9. At 5 am 2/Lieutenant Scott prepared to repeat the patrol taking another of 2/Lieutenant Davies-Scourfield's scout platoon sections with him under the command of Corporal Bill Gorringe to renew contact with the Germans.

SecondLieutenant Scott's carriers were seen by Munby's men as they passed Fort Nieulay at about 5 am and disappeared from view as they entered Coquelles. A short while later the garrison heard the sound of gunfire coming from the direction of the village. This time the carriers did not return immediately. At that point the Germans began the first of their assaults on the fort. Positioned along the ramparts and on the two northern bastions the British troops sought shelter from the German bombardment which began in earnest at 5.00 am and then watched anxiously as German infantry of the 86 Rifle Regiment emerged from a wood north of Coquelles to attack the fort. Rifleman Lyme on top of the north-west bastion, remembered his feelings on being in combat for the first time.

> 'It started with rifle and machine gun fire which...gave me a detached and semi thrilling interest in finding myself in the sounds of war without apparently any real danger. I was brought suddenly and horribly to reality when my left hand neighbour, incautiously raised his head and had his face virtually sliced in two by a machine gun burst.'

A few shells began to fall around Munby's position and he noticed the German infantry begin to move diagonally across his front over open ground in the direction of the sea. He was keen to let them advance until they were within weapon range and he passed these orders along to his men. Unfortunately, the French troops occupying the south-west bastion, were not as patient and opened fire almost immediately with their two heavy mitrailleuses. The Germans immediately went to ground and stayed down for half an hour, after which they scurried for the safety of the wood one by one. German casualties would have been light at that range if indeed they sustained any at all, and now the element of surprise had been

German machine gun team operating a MG34. TAYLOR LIBRARY

squandered. From the corner of the wood a German machine gun opened up on the fort and although it did no damage the searching fingers of tracer rounds indicated that the French machine gun emplacement had been located. A lone German sniper fired on the fort from a farm 400 yards to the front but was silenced by several bursts from a Bren gun. From then on the pounding increased and became so severe that Munby ordered all except one Bren into the shelters beneath the ramparts. As Tom Shewring had the No 1 Bren, he and Edward Lyme along with Lieutenant Nelson and the platoon Sergeant Ernie Osborne, installed it on the top of the north-west bastion.

In response, the French guns at Fort Lapin and the Bastion de l'Estran, which had been turned inland, fired on the German artillery. Those at Fort Lapin began firing at 5.30 am at Cap Blanc Nez and later concentrated their fire on the cross roads in Coquelles, but by 11.00 am they had used all their ammunition and orders were given for the guns to be spiked.

From their perch atop the battlements Munby and his men looked on as a lone scout carrier appeared from the direction of Coquelles and made the return journey towards the KRRC lines. There was no sign of the rest of 2/Lieutenant Scott's patrol. A little after 7 am rations were being handed around amongst a gloomy party of 'B' Company 2KRRC at bastion 9. There had been no sign of Scott's patrol and they feared the worst. Shortly afterwards a solitary Bren-gun carrier was seen coming slowly down the main road towards them. It pulled in near Company HQ and stopped. 2/Lieutenant Davies-Scourfield witnessed its return.

Davies-Scourfield

'Out of it jumped 'old' Bateman (aged about 35 and the most elderly member of my platoon) calling urgently for help. In front of the carrier, slumped beside his Boys rifle, sat Lance Corporal Smith, dead: beside him, exhausted and in pain, was the driver, Wilson, with a huge jagged wound in one leg. Blood was everywhere, and the armoured plating on the front of the vehicle was twisted and mangled. Bateman reported that the patrol, advancing down the main road had suddenly come under fire: they had tried to outflank the enemy by manoeuvring in the vehicles, but the two leading carriers, commanded by Dick and Corporal Gorringe, had been put out of action and, he thought, their crews all killed. He himself had opened fire with his Bren gun: then his carrier was also hit, but they had somehow managed to get back.'

Ron Savage noticed that the carrier had taken a direct hit from something like a two pounder anti-tank shell which had entered through the plating at the front and gone straight through the crew compartment. 'Ginger' Smith had been sitting directly in the line of fire in the seat Savage would have occupied.

Understandably downhearted at this unwelcome news the KRRC men got on with their tasks amid occasional shell bursts, certain that their comrades were lost.

Half an hour earlier at 6.30 am, however, Dick Scott had appeared at the Dauphine Gate of Fort Nieulay with another Rifleman. Scott had a bad flesh wound in his leg and a neat bullet hole through the rim of his tin hat and both men were exhausted from their ordeal. He was taken to Capitaine Herremann's office from where he reported the loss of his carriers by telephone. He then set off on foot for Calais and did not arrive at 2KRRC positions until 9.30 am when he reported that the crews of his and Corporal Gorringe's carriers were either dead or severely wounded. Scott had leapt from his carrier when it was hit and had taken cover at the side of the road from where he had shot one German with his pistol. He had then escaped by crawling back for several hundred yards along a water -filled ditch.

The Germans now began to bring mortar and artillery fire to bear on the fort and casualties began to mount. The wounded were taken down into a cellar below the north-west bastion and were attended to by Lance-Corporal Butler.

Sergeant Osborne decided he would take over on the Bren on the north west bastion and surprised his comrades by apparently ignoring the dictum of 'always short bursts' which he had spent months drilling into the rest of them. Sergeant Osborne, however, fired six magazines straight off with his finger tight on the trigger and as a result the barrel became red hot. A fully trained Bren Number Two, on hearing the command 'change barrels' could do it in six seconds, but that was according to the book and Sergeant Osborne had just thrown the book away. Edward Lyme was Number Two.

'" Change Barrels", called Ernie. Easy. I had spare barrels beside me and with the professionalism of long practice flipped up the catch and slid the barrel forward. But it wouldn't slide forward. The bloody thing wouldn't come off. It was too hot. I tugged and swore but to no avail...We got the thing down into a hollow and Ernie and I sat on the ground holding opposite ends of the Bren with our feet together tugging at the thing and laughing like a couple of schoolboys.'

At 11am 2/Lieutenant Davies-Scourfield at Bastion 9 picked up almost continuous muzzle flashes on the ridge above Coquelles and reported the positions back to HQ. Munby himself saw more German guns moving up but when he tried to communicate the positions of the German guns to HQ he found the lines broken by shell fire. There would be no further contact with Calais. A little later the Germans witnessed the arrival of the RAF to

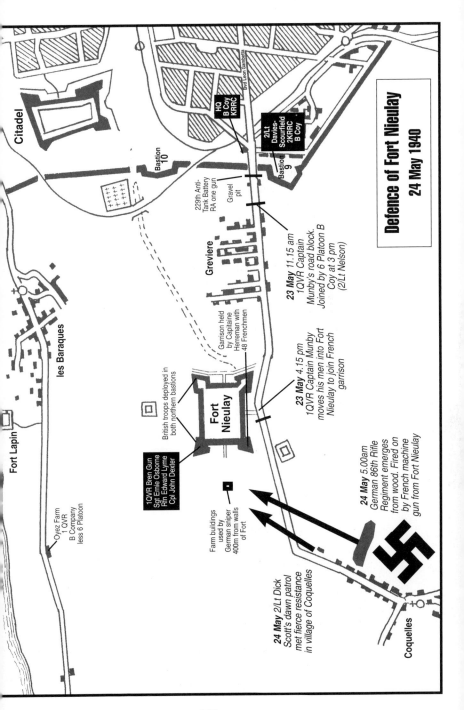

**Defence of Fort Nieulay
24 May 1940**

Citadel

Fort Lapin

les Baraques

Oyez Farm
1 QVR
B Company
less 6 Platoon

Bastion 10

Greviere

Bastion 9

Bvd Leon Gambetta

HQ
B Coy
KRRC

2/Lt
Davies-
Scourfield
2KRRC
B Coy

229th Anti-
Tank Battery
RA one gun

Gravel
pit

23 May 11.15 am
1QVR Captain
Munby's road block.
Joined by 6 Platoon B
Coy at 3 pm
(2/Lt Nelson)

Garrison held
by Capitaine
Herreman with
48 Frenchmen

British troops deployed in
both northern bastions

23 May 4.15 pm
1QVR Captain Munby
moves his men into Fort
Nieulay to join French
garrison

Fort
Nieulay

1QVR Bren Gun
Sgt Ernie Osborne
Rfn Edward Lyme
Cpl John Dexter

Farm buildings
used by
German sniper
400m from walls
of Fort

24 May 5.00am
German 86th Rifle
Regiment emerges
from wood. Fired on
by French machine
gun from Fort Nieulay

24 May 2/Lt Dick
Scott's dawn patrol
met fierce resistance
in village of Coquelles

Coquelles

devastating effect

> *'The English flyers arrive in broad daylight, first three 'Spitfires'. The whole day the Englishmen approach. Fighter, scout planes and again bombers. It is a damned short way, a jump over the Channel! Bombs crackle down. They plaster the streets ahead and the battery positions. Our 2cm AA gun fires as much as the barrels are able to deliver, three English planes are downed. Hardly a flight has dropped its bombs when another approaches. We suffer casualties.* **Now we know, the Englishman defends Calais.***'*

At noon the German bombardment slackened and Corporal Dexter reported to Captain Munby that a section of men near the Calais gate, feeling the position hopeless, were preparing to make a break back into town. As Munby and Lieutenant Nelson made their way across the open ground to try and stabilize the situation, a shell burst close by, knocking them flat. The men at the gate disappeared and were never seen again.

Rifleman Fletcher had been sent back on his motorcycle to ask for supplies and was ordered to act as a guide to escort a convoy of three carriers of 'C' Company of 2KRRC under 2/Lieutenant Pardoe up to Fort Nieulay. The plan was that Pardoe's convoy would meet Fletcher on the Sangatte road from where he would lead them south down a track to the fort. The rendezvous never took place. Pardoe decided to press on but one of his carriers became stuck in a ditch and he ordered another to stop and

A patrol of British troops in Bren gun carriers look out for signs of approaching Germans.

pull it out as he went on alone.

'I stopped about thirty yards from the Fort wondering whether the entrance was to the right or left. There was no sign of life. No sound. Suddenly my driver, a Rifleman Payne, pointed at some bushes to our front and there, unmistakably, was the barrel of a machine-gun pointed straight at us. The question was, who lay behind it? This was soon answered by a German soldier jumping up, crossing the track and lying down out of sight in a ditch across the road. There was an oath in my ear, from my machine-gunner, "Bugger, I had the safety catch on."' IWM 82/37/1

Pardoe felt that this was no time to hang around. He believed Nieulay had already fallen and it was time to return. He turned in his tracks and his small force spread out across the fields and made for 'home' as small arms fire opened up from the fort and mortar bombs began to fall around them.

At the German command post in the small wood to the right of the main street from where the infantry had assaulted earlier the commanders were considering their options. The storm troops' attack on the positions of 'B' and 'C' Companies of 2KRRC had faltered and they had been surprised by the amount of fire they had received. The artillery spotters were in position in the wood and the decision was made to put down the resistance with 'heavy weapons.' The Germans renewed their bombardment at 2 o'clock in the afternoon with increased venom.

The French 25mm gun at the main gate was hit without a shot being fired and Corporal John Dexter, with Riflemen Reg Dooley, Alec Dicker and Eric Barraball, plugged the gap. A direct hit on one of the two French heavy machine guns atop the south-west bastion killed and wounded several of the French detachment. John Dexter himself was later knocked off his feet with Sergeant John Moore. Dexter got up, Moore didn't. At that point amid the fury of the shellfire, a bizarre yet courageous vignette was played out.

Philip Pardoe

A French civilian in a truck drove up to the gate and reported to Captain Munby that a badly wounded British soldier was lying out on the road to Coquelles. The bravery of this unknown French civilian was an example to all as he offered to drive back and pick up the soldier if men could be spared to help lift him into his truck. While the driver was talking to Munby, John Dexter began to lift Sergeant Moore's body into the back of the truck Captain Munby approached him and told him what the civilian had said.

'We heard that a British soldier, badly wounded was in a farmhouse down the road. Bob Gibbs and I took the truck and its driver down the Boulogne Road and collected him (a KRRC Corporal well bandaged around

neck and chest). We loaded him into the truck beside John Moore and on the return trip, we jumped off and ran back into our position and the truck went to the hospital in Calais.'

It is possible that the corporal in question was Bill Gorringe as it was rumoured in 5 platoon that he had been hit in the chest by a machine gun burst. It is possible that he was taken into Calais in the truck but what is certain is that Bill Gorringe was killed at Calais, his date of death being recorded as 25 May, the day after Dick Scott's patrol. The body of Bill Gorringe, whose only wish had been to stay in England long enough to see his wife give birth to their child, was never found.

The bombardment which began at 2 pm was the prelude to another attack which was launched at 2.45 p.m. when light and heavy tanks advanced from Coquelles. Shells from the Panzers and from the artillery on the high ground began to smash into the brick curtain walls and rained down onto the glacis in front of them. Many shells fell inside the fort itself and the weight of the bombardment caused cracks to appear in the ceilings of the cellars beneath the bastions. Captain Munby narrowly escaped death again when a shell buried itself into an earth bank a few feet above him.

By 3.30 pm the German artillery fire had reached a crescendo and heavy artillery and mortar shells were falling inside the fort itself, but their fire had been matched by that of the guns of Allied warships operating just off the coast.

It was clear to Munby by now that the defence of Nieulay had reached a critical point. Even at this late stage Sergeant Ernie Osborne remained at his post in a hollow at the top of a mound on the north-west bastion firing his Bren gun. At around 4 pm the German troops had advanced to within one hundred yards of the walls under cover of a concentrated mortar barrage and just before 4.30 pm Captain Munby went to visit Capitaine Herremann in his underground HQ. Herremann had reached the conclusion that the fort was surrounded. He had made up his mind to surrender. Minutes later a white flag was hoisted on the flagpole, the gate was thrown open and German troops poured into the inner courtyard shouting at the men to drop their weapons. Corporal John Dexter and Rifleman Edward Lyme recalled their feelings at the moment they were taken prisoner.

'Imagine yourself to be in a crowded bus with solid tyres going all out across a rough and bumpy field and then to be struck by a train! That is how I felt. A mixture of emotions, shock, bewilderment, unreality – yet it is happening – and I am here. Why? What has gone wrong? Who surrendered? So that is what Jerry looks like close up! What happens now? How come the lads to the right are still firing? Hasn't the French Commander told them he has surrendered? (I drop the chamber of my revolver into

John Dexter

104

Germans finally overcame the resistance at Fort Nieulay and streamed in to capture the defenders.

the bushes and tear up letters addressed to me at our base in Kent.) Why had the idea of becoming a prisoner never occured to me? Why no advice or guidance? I feel worn out. I wonder how we will get out of this?'

'The Germans streamed into the fort and surrounded the entrance to the cellar ordering us out. ...I took my revolver out of my holster (for the first time!) With my finger on the trigger but with my hands in the air I came out into daylight. It was ridiculous, and I have no idea what I intended to do... A young German holding a Schmeisser indicated that a pistol was not desirable and I meekly pulled my lanyard over my head and handed it to him.'

One of the 'lads to the right' was Sergeant Osborne but as more Germans swept into the fort the firing from the top of the north-west bastion stopped. Sergeant Osborne came down from his position and told John Dexter that he had thrown his Bren gun over the parapet for fear of reprisals. Fort Nieulay had fallen. The white flag was taken down and the Swastika was hoisted in its place signalling its capture to the German commanders. As the men were herded out of the fort on to the road they witnessed a steady stream of German tanks, infantry and artillery swarming down the hill from Coquelles and moving up towards Calais. They also saw the bodies of stricken German soldiers still writhing and kicking on the ground, a sign of the bitter struggle for Nieulay.

REFCE. CAS /5/ 1479
No.......................................

(If replying, please quote above No.)

Army Form B. 104—83.

Rifle Record Office,

WINCHESTER. Station.

15th July 1940

SIR ~~OR MADAM,~~

I have to inform you that a report has been receive from the War Office to the effect that (No.) 6896661

(Rank) Rfn. (Name) John Edward Dexter

(Regiment) 1st. Q.V.R

is a Prisoner of War

Should any other information be received concerning him, such information will be at once communicated to you.

Instructions as to the method of communicating with Prisoners of War can be obtained at any Post Office.

I am,

SIR ~~OR MADAM,~~

Your obedient Servant,

[signature] Major

for Officer in charge of Records.

IMPORTANT.—Any change of your address should be immediately notified to this Office. It should also be notified, if you receive information from the soldier above, that his address has been changed.

Wt.30241/1250 500M. 9/39. KJL/8818 Gp.698/3 Forms/B.104—83A/6

A mixed bag of prisoners, French and British, captured by units of Guderian's Korps march off to captivity.

As Corporal Dexter was lined up on the road with the rest of the garrison, officers were being rounded up for questioning.

The determined defence of Vauban's old fort had succeeded in obstructing the advance of the Germans up the Boulogne road towards the heart of Calais for the best part of twelve hours. Now, with Nieulay out of the way, the Panzers were free to advance unimpeded across country towards 'B' Company 1QVR at Oyez Farm and against the western face of the outer perimeter.

Parties of German infantry had by-passed Fort Nieulay to attack 'B' Company 2KRRC at around 11.30 am and half an hour later a squadron of German medium Panzers deployed in two long lines began to crawl down from the Coquelles ridge. They too by-passed the fort and supported their infantry in attacking both the left and right flanks of 'B' Company. The Germans fought their way into the Cimetière Nord, less than one hundred metres from the ramparts held by 'C' Company 2KRRC but were driven out by a counter attack from a section under Sergeant Dryborough-Smith which had been sent forward by 2/Lieutenant Philip Pardoe.

In the early afternoon the Germans pressed their attack with tanks and the forward posts were eventually driven out of their positions in the houses and gardens in front of Bastion 9 after first destroying two German light tanks. Bullets chipped pieces off the concrete blocks behind which the riflemen sheltered and the leading tank destroyed one of the anti-tank guns of 229 battery at a road block just to the right of Bastion 9. It then proceeded to demolish the barricade with gunfire. More German tanks darted among the houses and gardens and sprayed Bastion 9 with machine gun fire.

107

Davies-Scourfield replied with mortars and Brens. It was a fierce struggle and Lieutenant Colonel Miller, fearing for the stability of his line, sent up reinforcements of fifty men of the Searchlights under Lieutenant Airey Neave. Neave met Major Poole on the railway tracks at the Pont Jourdan railway bridge who told him that there was possibility of a German break through. After telling Neave to get his men into houses on either side of the bridge and fire from the windows he concluded by saying '...you must fight like bloody hell.'

By 8 pm the Germans were only 200 metres from 2/Lieutenant Davies-Scourfield's position firing machine gun bullets and tank shells straight down the Boulevard Léon Gambetta, knocking chunks of masonry from the houses and smashing windows. Soon after, however, just as the light began to fade, the noise of battle died down and the pressure on 'B' Company eased. They had withstood the fury of the German attack. Meanwhile 'B' Company of 1 QVR and the gunners of 6 Heavy Anti-Aircraft Battery out at Oyez Farm had been forced back towards Calais along the coast road after the fall of Fort Nieulay. Second Lieutenant Dizer had tried unsuccessfully to blow up the submarine cable at Sangatte with hand grenades and had only just escaped. As the Territorials retired they were attacked by three RAF Bristol Blenheims returning from a bombing run against the German guns on the Coquelles ridge and two riflemen were wounded. They reached the ramparts held by the men of 'C' Company 2KRRC, with whom they would fight from then on, at 10 pm that night. At Bastion 9 there descended an eerie silence. Davies-Scourfield's men felt they had acquitted themselves well and as they waited they wondered when the Germans would try again.

German troops manning a 3.7cm Pak 35/36 anti-tank gun. Dubbed the *Heeresanklopfgerät* (army door knocking gear) by them because of its failure to penetrate French and British armour.

CHAPTER TEN

IF THEY WANT CALAIS THEY'LL HAVE TO FIGHT FOR IT

By the late afternoon of 24 May the situation on the west and south-west perimeter had become critical and it became clear that the defensive line in that area could not be held for another day. Brigadier Nicholson, who was in his HQ only 600 metres from the Pont Jourdan on the Boulevard Léon Gambetta, made the decision to withdraw to a line of posts which stretched across the centre of Calais St. Pierre. Preparations were also put in hand to withdraw by stages to the line of the canals and Bassins surrounding Calais Nord and to defend the three bridges which spanned them. Major 'Puffin' Owen, Second in Command 2KRRC was put in charge of the defence of the bridges. The three bridges – Pont Freycinet, Pont Richelieu (Georges V) and Pont Faidherbe – were to witness some of the bitterest street fighting of the entire battle. These bridges were never destroyed thereby reducing 30 Brigade's ability to defend the inner perimeter. In the end the defenders had to resort to barricading the bridges and streets. Later that evening Brigadier Nicholson moved his HQ from the Clinique on the Boulevard Léon Gambetta to the Gare Maritime, the site of the present-day ferry terminal.

From 8 pm onwards the ominous rattle of German tank tracks could be heard moving up through the streets of south-west St. Pierre as the British withdrew to their next line of defence. With the withdrawal to the inner perimeter the defence of Calais took on an even more desperate air. With

A PzKpfw Mk III rattles through a street with houses well alight all around.

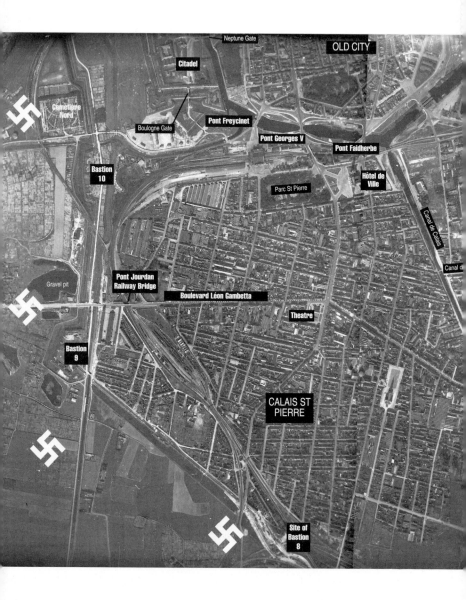

Neptune Gate

OLD CITY

Citadel

Cimetière
Nord

Pont Freycinet

Boulogne Gate

Pont Georges V

Pont Faidherbe

**Bastion
10**

**Hôtel de
Ville**

Parc St Pierre

Canal de Calais

Canal d

Gravel pit

**Pont Jourdan
Railway Bridge**

Boulevard Léon Gambetta

Theatre

**Bastion
9**

**CALAIS ST
PIERRE**

**Site of
Bastion
8**

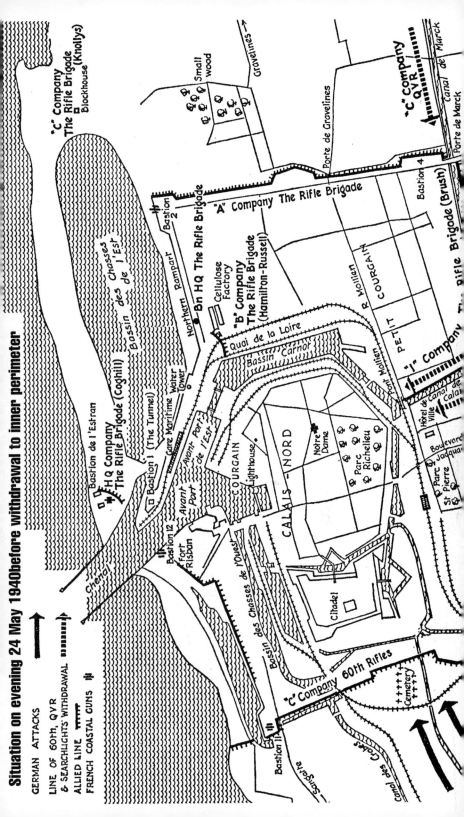

Situation on evening 24 May 1940 before withdrawal to inner perimeter

GERMAN ATTACKS ➤
LINE OF 60th, QVR & SEARCHLIGHTS WITHDRAWAL ▪▪▪▪▪➤
ALLIED LINE ┬┬┬┬┬
FRENCH COASTAL GUNS ⚒

"C" Company The Rifle Brigade (Knollys)
Blockhouse
Small wood
Gravelines →
"C" Company QVR
Porte de Gravelines
Canal de Marck
Porte de Marck
Bastion 4
"A" Company The Rifle Brigade
Bastion 2
Bastion des Chasses de l'Est
Bassin des Chasses de l'Est
Northern Rampart
Bn HQ The Rifle Brigade
Cellulose Factory
"B" Company The Rifle Brigade (Hamilton-Russell)
R. Mollien
COURGAIN
PETIT
"I" Company The Rifle Brigade (Brush)
Bastion de l'Estran
HQ Company The Rifle Brigade (Coghill)
Bastion I (The Tunnel)
Gare Maritime
Water Tower
Quai de la Loire
Bassin Carnot
Pont Mollien
Canal de Calais
Hôtel de Ville
Chenal
Bastion 12
Fort Risban
Avant Port de l'Est
COURGAIN
Avant Port de l'Ouest
lighthouse
Notre Dame
Parc Richelieu
CALAIS — NORD
St Pierre
Parc St Pierre
Boulevard Jacquard
Bastion 11
Citadel
Bassin des Chasses de l'Ouest
Canal de la Sauvette
"C" Company 60th Rifles
Cemetery
Canal des

their backs to the sea many of the defenders still believed evacuation a possibility but it was not to be.

Soon after dawn on Saturday, 25 May, Major Owen crossed the Pont Faidherbe in a car and moved slowly down the main streets of St. Pierre. He reported no signs of the Germans. At 5.30 am and again at 7 am, however, tentative patrols under Major Peter Brush of 1 RB, by now withdrawn to and holding a precarious salient bounded by the Canal de Marck and the eastern face of the outer perimeter from Bastion 2 to Bastion 4, crossed the Pont Mollien, saw armed German motorcyclists in the Boulevard Léon Gambetta and fired on German Officers lining civilians up

for interrogation outside the Hôtel de Ville. Peter Brush was wounded in the throat by a sniper at 8.00 am near the Pont Mollien. He refused to leave his HQ until he received a direct order to do so from Lieutenant Colonel Hoskyns himself. At the same time the men of 1 RB and those of 2 KRRC holding the waterfront from Pont Freycinet to the bridge over the canal leading to the Place de Norvège groaned as the Swastika inched its way up the flag pole of the Hôtel de Ville and fluttered in the breeze. The Germans could now observe all movements around the areas of the waterfront and the bridges.

From the Hôtel de Ville today it takes just a few minutes to walk to the centre bridge, the Pont Georges V but in 1940, when it was known as Pont Richelieu and was being held by elements of 'D' Company 2 KRRC under Major Lord Godfrey Cromwell, the men of the 60th Rifles determined to make the Germans fight every inch of the way. The same determination was evident at the other bridges and on the eastern front held by 1RB. At each of the bridges road blocks were constructed using every abandoned vehicle available and barricades were set up across the streets leading from the canal line.

Almost every house overlooking the waterfront along the Quai de l'Escaut, the Quai de la Tamise and the Quai de la Meuse was turned into a defensive position as were the houses on the streets from the Place d'Angleterre east to the canal where the platoons of 'B' Company, 2KRRC were scattered. This was no easy task as the houses had first to be broken into and then cleared of all civilians and unarmed French and Belgian troops. Throughout, the defenders faced the ever present dangers of Fifth Columnists and German snipers who had succeeded in infiltrating Calais-Nord and had then begun to fire on the British from the rear. It was later claimed that one of them had taken up a position atop the roof of the Church of Notre Dame on the Rue Notre Dame with a sub machine gun, a position perilously close to Lieutenant

With the Germans in possession of the Hotel de Ville snipers could use the clock tower to pick off defenders manning the barricades.

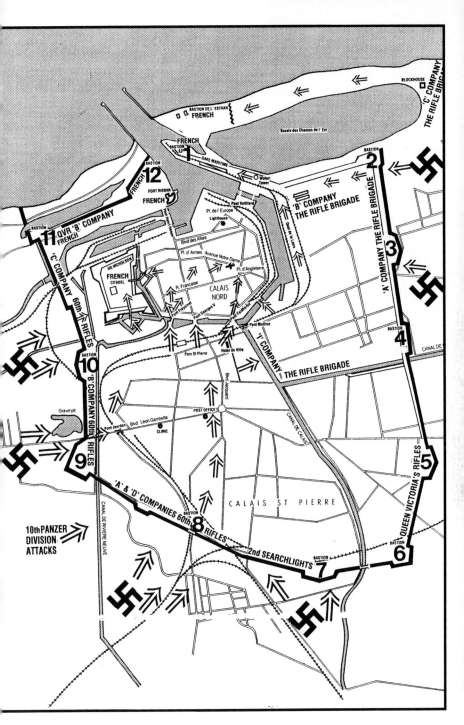

BLOCKHOUSE

'C' COMPANY
THE RIFLE BRIG...

Bastin des Chasses de l' Est

BASTION DE L' ESTRAN
FRENCH

BASTION 1
FRENCH

GARE MARITIME

Water Tower

BASTION 2
'A' COMPANY THE RIFLE BRIGADE

BASTION 12
FORT RISBAN
FRENCH

FRENCH

'B' COMPANY
THE RIFLE BRIGADE

Pont Vetillard

Pt. de l' Europe

Lighthouse

Quai de la Loire

BASTION 3

BASTION 11
QVR 'B' COMPANY
FRENCH

Blvd des Allies

Pt. d'Armes Avenue Notre Dame

'C' COMPANY 60th RIFLES

HQ NICHOLSON

FRENCH
CITADEL

R. Francaise

Pt. d'Angleterre

CALAIS
NORD

Pont Freycinet

Pont Georges V

Pont Faidherbe

Pont Mollien

BASTION 4

CANAL DE

'I' COMPANY

THE RIFLE BRIGADE

Parc St Pierre

Hotel de Ville

BASTION 10

'B' COMPANY 60th RIFLES

Gravel pit

Pont Jourdan

POST OFFICE

Blvd Jacquard

CANAL DE CALAIS

Blvd Leon Gambetta

CLINIC

BASTION 9

'A' & 'D' COMPANIES 60th RIFLES

CALAIS ST PIERRE

QUEEN VICTORIA'S RIFLES

BASTION 5

10th PANZER
DIVISION
ATTACKS

CANAL DE RIVIERE NEUVE

BASTION 8

2nd SEARCHLIGHTS

BASTION 7

BASTION 6

General Schall

Colonel Miller's HQ in the Rue du Duc de Guise. Other German snipers took up positions in the clock tower of the Hôtel de Ville and made all movement around the bridge areas and along the waterfront extremely hazardous, particularly for junior officers and NCO's attempting to keep in touch with their men. The psychological impact of being under fire from all sides and not knowing where the bullets were coming from jangled the nerves of all the riflemen, however.

At 11 am the men of 'D' Company 2KRRC saw an armoured vehicle displaying a white flag, approach the southern end of Pont Richelieu. General Schall, commanding 10 Panzer Division, was about to launch an all-out attack on the inner perimeter and the Citadel with every available gun and with dive bomber support. Before that he tried to take Calais without a fight.

He had estimated his division to be at a little over half its strength when it reached Calais and after the hard fighting and heavy RAF attacks of the previous day it had been further weakened. Schall had been told in no uncertain terms the previous afternoon by Guderian that if losses were heavy the attack should only be continued with support from the Luftwaffe and heavy artillery. Schall was to avoid 'unnecessary losses' at all costs.

At the Hôtel de Ville the Mayor of Calais, Andre Gershell, had been captured whilst he was working at his desk. The Germans decided to send him to see Brigadier Nicholson to ask for the formal surrender of the British and French forces. Gershell was escorted to the Citadel where Nicholson had by then established his HQ in the heavily sandbagged north-east bastion to be in touch with the French Army commander Commandant Le Tellier. Lieutenant

Andre Gershell

Austin Evitts had accompanied Brigadier Nicholson on his journey to the Citadel at 4.30 am that morning and witnessed the meeting.

'Sometime around 0900 hours a surprise visitor was brought to the Citadel. He was a civilian and blindfolded. The visitor, I was told, was the

114

Brigadier Nicholson

*Mayor of Calais and he had come with a message from the German commander. It was in the courtyard of the quadrangle where the Brigadier received him and the message was an ultimatum. If he had not surrendered in 24 hours, the Germans had said, Calais would be bombed and shelled and razed to the ground and the Mayor was making a special plea, he said, to save the town from further destruction and loss of life."Surrender," said the Brigadier in a decidedly brusque manner, "No I shall not surrender. Tell the Germans that **if they want Calais they will have to fight for it.**"*

His words were spoken loudly and clearly, and standing only a few yards away near the wireless truck I heard them quite distinctly.'

Nicholson's refusal to surrender was the signal for an incredibly ferocious bombardment of the Citadel and Fort Risban. From the Citadel to Fort Risban the shells screamed down on the defenders. At the roadblocks and in the houses along the waterfront machine gun bullets thudded into the vehicles and furniture at the windows and barricades and whined crazily off walls and pavements. At the Pont Mollien, mortar bombs set fire to the bridge and Stuka dive bombers terrorized 1RB behind the Canal de Marck.

At 2.15 pm Nicholson received the message from Eden which was considered so momentous by Lieutenant Evitts that he scribbled it down word for word in his diary even though the Citadel was under attack. The day after 'Empire Day' Nicholson was told that the defence of Calais to the 'utmost' was vital to show continued co-operation with France and that 'the eyes of the whole Empire' were on him and his men. It was the first indication that evacuation might not happen. An hour later Schall once more attempted to force Nicholson into surrender and sent Leutnant Hoffman of 2 Battalion, 69 Rifle Regiment across the Pont Richelieu with the message. Hoffman was taken up the Rue Royale to the Neptune gate of the Citadel. He delivered Schall's demand of the immediate surrender of the Citadel otherwise, he promised, the whole of Calais-Nord was to be levelled. There was an eerie lull in the fighting as Hoffman awaited Nicholson's reply. With the words of Eden's signal still fresh in his mind the Brigadier wrote down his response and handed it to Hoffman. 'The answer is no,' it read 'as it is the British Army's duty to fight as well as it is the German's.'

Hoffman re-crossed the bridge at 4.35 pm and the battle resumed. The

Germans crossing Pont Henri Henon.

Germans applied more pressure, particularly on 1RB and 'C' and 'D' Companies of 1 QVR which had by then withdrawn through the RB from their outlying positions beyond the outer perimeter. With 2KRRC fighting hard along the line of the canal and the bridges, 1QVR retired along the Quai de la Loire and the southern shore of the Bassin des Chasses de l'Est, first towards the northern ramparts and then on to the narrow neck of land which is now the site of the ferry terminal. It would be on that strip of land, with only the sea behind them, where 1RB and 1 QVR would make their final stand. Meanwhile 'A' Company of 1RB under Major Taylor and 'I' Company were gradually forced back from their posts on the eastern ramparts and the Canal de Marck. Major Taylor was wounded in fierce hand to hand fighting with the German 69 Rifle Regiment which took place in the back streets between the Bassin Carnot and the outer perimeter. He retired to Battalion HQ situated in a trench near Bastion 1 at 3.30 pm and as he was asking Lieutenant Colonel Hoskyns for reserves to go and rescue some RB men cut off in the Rue Mollien, a shell burst in the trench sending a splinter into Lieutenant Colonel Hoskyns' side and wounding Taylor for a second time.

At 3.30 pm on the afternoon of Saturday 25 May, just before he received that fatal wound from a shell splinter, Lieutenant Colonel Hoskyns had agreed that a counter attack should be made along the Quai de la Loire by elements of 'I' Company under the already wounded Major Brush. Their mission was to rescue the men trapped in the Rue Mollien. Some seventeen men moved forward past a RB road block commanded by Major Hamilton-Russell, but intense fire stopped them in their tracks. Out of the swarm of bullets a French truck raced towards them driven by a man in a Belgian uniform. Sitting beside him with a pistol to the man's head was Corporal Lane of 'I' Company. Lane had arrested the man as a suspected Fifth Columnist and had seen to it that the truck had been loaded with 'I' Company wounded before forcing the captured man to drive back to the RB lines. When the truck was hit and slewed to a halt 2/Lieutenant Edward Bird ran forward and tried to restart it. At this point Bird was shot in the head and Major Brush and his men raced across to the truck, pulled the wounded from the blazing vehicle and dragged them back to the British positions. Second Lieutenant Bird managed to stagger back with them but died of his wounds half an hour later.

C B A Chandos Hoskyns

'A' Company, although involved in bitter fighting on three sides during its withdrawal from the ramparts and suffering many casualties as a result, was still fighting as a unit. Platoon Sergeant Major (PSM) Richard Johnston, known to all as 'Sybil', had taken a position near the road block on the Rue Mollien which Rifleman Sandford of 2KRRC had helped to build on 23 May, in order to cover the rear of 'A' Company HQ. Doug Wheeler was sent up to join him.

'There were seven of us in all, including Corporal Berryman, another DR. The block was made out of these big rolls of undersea cable. It was a pretty solid effort. The firing seemed to be getting closer and more heavy. Down the road we could see huge fires burning. A little while later we got a visit from Major Brush. We used to call him "Maggie". He was a great bloke, a popular officer; anyone would have been proud to have known him. He was wounded in the throat and he had a first aid dressing round it and two fingers missing from one hand. He told us, "You will soon come under fire and I want you to hold this position for as long as possible. It is imperative that you hold it, even to the last man." Well one of the old

117

*soldiers went round us saying, "Eeny, meeny, miny mo". The 'old sweats',
they never lost their sense of humour!*

*All down the Rue Mollien there were civilians and British soldiers
crossing the road from one side towards the docks side and there was a lot
of firing going on. We were getting a fair 'smack' into the barricade. Sybil
said we should fire as hard as we could at the tops of the buildings to
prevent the Germans from shooting the people crossing the road. Sybil had
a telescope and said that one of the soldiers trying to cross the road was
wounded. He was crawling because he couldn't stand up. He told us to
charge down the road and bring him in but the old soldiers were not stupid
and were not keen to go. Sybil was disgusted with this and said "Cover
me,"and he took the wheelbarrow we'd been using to make the road block
and ran out down the road. Berryman watched him through the telescope
through a chink in the barricade and Sybil staggered and staggered and
staggered and that was it, he stopped half way down the road. He should
have got a medal, he was a great bloke. I met a rifleman as a POW named
Hills and he said he'd been wounded and kept behind after treatment and he
was with a party of Germans who were sent out to find the bodies and bury
them. He said PSM Johnston was lying in the wheelbarrow and it was
almost full of blood. He must have been hit about a dozen times'.*

By 4.30 pm the Citadel appeared to those observers who could see it, to be
enveloped by a great wall of flame and from 6.30 pm another terrific
artillery and mortar bombardment pounded the British in the Citadel and
around the bridges, the fire being directed from the tower of the Hôtel de
Ville. On 'B' Company 2KRRC's front near Place de Norvège, Jack Poole
sent around the latest message from Lieutenant Colonel Miller. 'Present
positions will be held at all costs to the last round and to the last man.' At
around 7.30 pm the bombardment suddenly ceased and the rumble of
tracks heralded the appearance of German tanks at those three vital
bridges separating Calais-Nord from St. Pierre. Hubert Borchert recorded
the German cannonade.

*'A hot day the 25 May. There is heavy fighting for every inch of ground.
The Citadel of Calais must be shot ripe for the assault. Shell after shell roars
out of the German barrels towards the bunkers and heavy fortifications.
Heavy tank hunters, engineers with rafts, assault engineers, field howitzers
...and light AA for ground support of the rifle companies are drawn
forward. In the evening at 6.30 a surprising hurricane of fire. Hit after hit
crashes high over the Citadel and Fort Risban at the mouth of the harbour.
The officers look to their watches: ten minutes, five, now the firing stops!
The sudden silence is very impressive. It is 7.40. The storm troops advance
with much doggedness. The guns fire in open positions. The heavy and light
tank hunters and the 2 cm AA guns send shell after shell out of the quick
firing barrels. The infantry support guns and the trench mortars are*

The improvised barricade at the Pont Faidherbe and another on the Rue de Bruxelles, manned by B Company, 2KRRC. Note the German staff car on the pavement. this was the vehicle searched by Corporal Hunby and Rifleman Ewings, 1 am, 26 May. Note the group of prisoners walking towards the road block with hands raised

German attackers' eye view of the barricade at Pont Faidherbe.

British roadblock at the end of Rue des Thermes and the corner of Place d'Armes.

thumping. Riflemen and engineers jump forward, the machine gunners hammer as if crazy. All men are fiercely determined. Comrades fell, were wounded and others jump forward. There is only a slow advance. The adversary defends himself with the courage of despair. From all sides the German storm troops were fiercely fired upon. But they advance. They open passages in the west of the town by force, step by step'.

The Germans probed the bridges and were met with fierce resistance. At Pont Faidherbe on the left of the 2KRRC front three tanks followed by a saloon car began to force the British road block but were repulsed when two of the tanks and the car were hit on the German side of the bridge. Major Puffin Owen and several other Riflemen were killed during this attack.

At the centre bridge, Pont Richelieu, the first tank across triggered a mine and the attack faltered although the Germans kept up a heavy fire from houses along the Quai de Danube. The situation was most critical, however, at the right hand bridge, Pont Freycinet. Under cover of a heavy mortar barrage one tank forced the road block and was followed over by German infantry. Captain C Stanton immediately organized a counter-attack with two platoons of 'A' Company. Captain Stanton, who was in temporary command of 'A' Company due the hospitalization of Major Trotter with a head wound the day before, led the counter-attack himself. He had also been slightly wounded twice during 24 May in the heavy fighting on the southern face of the outer perimeter, but he nevertheless led his men against the Germans. During the assault he was hit by several high calibre bullets through the body and staggered back to report to Lieutenant Colonel Miller, only to fall unconscious at the CO's feet. His attack had succeeded in forcing the tank to retire but it had not been enough to dislodge German infantrymen who had succeeded in taking up firing positions in houses near the Citadel. At this point Major Trotter returned from hospital and tried to stabilize the line by establishing a line of posts from the Citadel down the streets to Pont Freycinet.

The withdrawal of 1RB had exposed the left flank of 2KRRC and had placed 'B' Company in the front line and although they had not been directly attacked, they had met the full force of the German bombardment and casualties had mounted. 2/Lieutenant Martin Willan was killed as was a rifleman who ran to his aid. Everyone was by now dog tired. 2/ Lieutenant Davies-Scourfield was ordered to check up on Lieutenant Richard Warre's platoon of 'D' Company 2KRRC to his right and find out why his men were blazing away over the canal. Davies-Scourfield found that Warre, an officer held in high regard by the men of his platoon, had fallen into a deep sleep out of sheer fatigue and without his guidance his men were heavily engaged in firing on German tanks which they swore they had seen moving along the Quai de la Moselle. Davies-Scourfield sent Warre's trusted Corporal Birt to stop them. Neither Warre nor his Corporal would survive the fighting next day. Moments later, outside 'B' Company HQ in the Place d'Angleterre, a weary Company Sergeant Major Rawlinson failed to respond to a sentry's challenge and in the total confusion wrought by close quarter combat was shot through both cheeks by one of his own men. Major Jack Poole witnessed the accident and noted that the sentry went, '...completely berserk and had to be restrained by a clout on the head with a rifle butt.'

As it began to grow dark the flames leaping from the burning buildings and fanned by a strengthening wind cast an eerie orange glow over the streets and barricades. The riflemen had little food or water – the water mains had been destroyed by the shelling – ammunition was scarce and men in reserve to provide relief were non-existent. Almost every man was in the front line. The heat, smoke and dust added to the riflemen's burdens. Casualties had been heavy and the battalions faced the prospect of fighting the next day with some 250 unwounded men each, with no tank, anti-tank or artillery support. They were, however, still undefeated. Hubert Borchert remarked that, in the evening the German infantry had, '...achieved the positions for the final assault west of the Citadel and in the south at the borders of the old town.' The Germans had breached the inner perimeter and were preparing to finish the job. Unfortunately, by then Doug Wheeler's part in the defence of Calais had come to an end through no fault of his own.

After witnessing the death of Sybil Johnston at the road block on the Rue Mollien, Wheeler's small party came under increasing fire and their ammunition was running low. At this point Corporal Berryman made a decision to withdraw towards the harbour.

'All we had left then was twenty full magazines for the Bren, the anti tank rifle with only two rounds left, we only had five to start with and Cpl. Berryman said,"I'm not going to ask you this time. Pack up, get yourselves organised, we're going back." We all did that and it was just dusk, the sun had set but it was still light. We loaded up and took off and raced down to this road that went along the canal and we ran right into what must have been four hundred unarmed Frenchmen all coming out of Bastion 3. They were shouting "No shoot, no shoot, la guerre fini", and all this sort of thing. They surrounded us and we sat down for a minute while Berryman tried to sort things out because we couldn't get through them. All of a sudden the way opened and up came some Germans, there must have been seven or eight of them, and they must have got as big a shock as we did. They were escorting these prisoners I suppose. Anyway there was nothing we could do we just put up our hands. They were very interested in our uniform and our weapons and the bloke in charge told us that we were the first British troops they had seen close up. One of them came up and he was pointing his machine pistol at me and poking it in my nose, so close I could almost see the bullets! He was screaming his head off and I hadn't got a clue what he

British and French prisoners taken during the battle. The PzKpfw II is transporting four English wounded soldiers.

Original German situation map belonging to the 10th Panzer Division showing the positions of its units during the final assault on the Old Town 26 May 1940.
BUNDESARCHIV FREIBURG

was talking about. Suddenly I thought it must have been the French bayonet I'd got stuck in my belt that he meant but I thought that if I made a grab at it he'd think I was going to stab him and if it was not that he was going to shoot me for sure. I didn't know what to do. Berryman said he wanted the bayonet and anyway the German made a grab at it, tore it out and threw it a mile away. Everything was quiet after that. That was Saturday night and as far as I was concerned that was the battle finished. We were the first prisoners actually. First they took us to a church which was on fire and they made us put our respirators and tin hats on the floor with our AB 64's (pay book) on top, then they made us turn round and face the wall with our hands on our heads. The only memory I have is one of utter relief that I was going to be out of it after all. They marched us off to a place called Marquise, down towards Cap Griz-Nez.'

The final act of Saturday 25 May was the dive-bombing of the few troops who remained to defend Bastion 2, but General Schall, convinced now that the British would fight on, decided to call a halt to the German attack at 9.45 pm. During the night the remaining British troops withdrew to their final positions. Messages received by Dover from Major Alexander Allan, by that time in command of 1RB in place of Lieutenant Colonel Hoskyns near the Gare Maritime, on that Saturday evening conveyed the gravity of the situation:

'Citadel a shambles stop Brigadier's fate unknown stop Rifle Brigade casualties unknown stop Being heavily shelled and flanked but attempting counter attack stop Am attempting contact with 60th fighting in the town

'For you the war is over!' A group of British prisoners captured at Calais. Note the smoke-blackened face of the man in the middle of the front rank.

stop Are you sending ships stop Quay intact in spite of very severe bombardment.'

At midnight Lieutenant Colonel Miller made his way to the Citadel to see Brigadier Nicholson but Nicholson was out visiting the troops as he had been doing all day. It was not until 1.30 am, 26 May, that Nicholson met Miller at Miller's HQ near the Parc Richelieu to discuss the situation. He also showed Miller a copy of Eden's fateful message. At almost the same time as Miller set out to see Brigadier Nicholson, Von Oberst Fischer, commanding officer of the German 10 Rifle Brigade, was moving his HQ into the fourth floor of the Theatre in the Place Albert 1er in St. Pierre and setting up his brigade observation post on the roof. Fischer was under no illusions about the British resistance and ordered artillery and AA guns to be moved up close to the bridges to support the attack which was to continue the next day. Despite the failure to take Calais on 25 May as the necessary preparations were completed Fischer and his troops counted the hours to the attack '...the success of which nobody calls into question.'

On the western front the Citadel was still being protected by a small, mixed force of 60th Rifles under Captain Everard Radcliffe and French soldiers and sailors under the command of Capitaine Michel de la Blanchardière in Bastion 11. The French soldiers and sailors inside Bastion 11 became known as 'The Volunteers of Calais', as they had responded to an appeal by the French Naval commander Carlos de Lambertye to stay and fight rather than be evacuated to safety on 24 May. Men like de Lambertye and de la Blanchardière have a special place in the hearts of the French since they, along with some 800 other French volunteers, fought to the last alongside the British forces.

After the French naval gunners in the coastal batteries had used all their ammunition on 24 May and had been ordered to spike their guns prior to evacuation, Carlos de Lambertye had realized that if all the seafront defences were abandoned simultaneously then the way to the Citadel would be left wide open. In defiance of French naval orders de Lambertye appealed to the sailors who had left their positions and were waiting at the docks for evacuation, to go back and defend the bastions. Capitaine Michel de la Blanchardière, a staff officer of the 21 French Infantry Division, had been the first man to step forward followed by the other volunteers. Instead of sailing away, these men stayed to hold

Carlos de Lambertye

125

The western wall of Fort Risban shortly after it fell.

the coastal defences. Carlos de Lambertye had his HQ at Fort Risban which had come under an incredible bombardment along with the Citadel and Bastion 12. Lambertye, an old and sick man, was later to die of a heart attack during the morning of 26 May as he made his way back across the Ponts Henri Hénon to his HQ in Fort Risban. He had already visited 1RB at the Gare Maritime, had personally visited his men in trenches near Fort Risban and had been to the Citadel. The strain of battle was telling on younger and fitter men and such was the tempo of the struggle in Calais that Lambertye's ailing heart simply could not cope.

At 3 am in the early hours of Sunday 26 May the small force in Bastion 11 was attacked, and four hours later Capitaine de la Blanchardière had been wounded severely. By 1 pm that Sunday afternoon, after a stand of some ten hours, the Germans finally took Bastion 11. Of the French contingent only seventeen were left alive and just thirty out of the eighty riflemen of 2 KRRRC were unwounded. The way to the Citadel was now open from the west.

* * * *

On the waterfront near the bridges there had been high drama at Pont Faidherbe during the early hours of Sunday morning. At 1am Lance Corporal Humby and Rifleman Ewings of Headquarters Company 2KRRC had risked their lives by volunteering to cross the bridge to search the abandoned German saloon car which had attempted to follow the German tank across the previous evening. The car was on the German held end of the bridge only fifty metres or so from a German post and the approaches were continually swept by fire. From under the noses of the sentries the riflemen took papers from the pockets of a dead German pioneer officer and re-crossed the bridge safely. The entire journey across the bridge and back, a distance of some sixty metres, had taken two hours.

It was around 5 am when Sergeant Wall woke 2/Lieutenant Davies-Scourfield out of his deep sleep in his cellar near the Place de Norvège. His men breakfasted sparingly on their remaining supplies of biscuits and bully beef and then 'with a stupendous roar', the whole of the German XIX Corps artillery opened up on 2KRRC holding the canal line, the Citadel and on Bastion 11 which by then had been under attack for two hours. The shelling increased in intensity from 7 am and from 9.30 am wave after wave of Stuka dive-bombers lashed Calais-Nord with high explosive and incendiary bombs, turning what was left of the old town into a raging furnace. At 9.15 am two German infantry companies attacked the lock between the Quai de la Volga and the Place de Norvège near 2/Lieutenant Davies-Scourfield's positions under cover of a mortar barrage and at the same time another infantry company had turned north and were fighting seaward along the Quai de la Loire, squeezing 1RB ever deeper onto the narrow neck of land towards the Gare Maritime and Bastion 1.

Amid the barrage Davies-Scourfield decided to try and make contact with other units of 'B' Company and as he made his way to Company HQ he met his friend 2/Lieutenant Dick Scott near the crossroads in the Place d'Angleterre. Scott told him the shocking news that Major Henry Scott, second in command of 'B' Company, had been hit and was dying. Dick Scott was on his way to find a truck to take him to an aid post. Davies-Scourfield hurried along to 'B' Company HQ and slid into the opening to the cellar. He helped Major Poole lift Major Scott from the cellar on a large blanket and laid him in the front passage of the house ready for 2/Lieutenant Scott's truck. 'Leave my tin hat on' were the last words uttered by Major Scott as his batman tried to remove it to make him more comfortable. Dick Scott appeared with a truck and backed it up to the door but almost at once the canopy was shredded by a machine gun burst and a rain of mortar shells began to fall. Seeing that Major Scott was dead Major Poole ordered everyone to make a dash for the next house. As bombs fell around them they climbed the partition wall and scurried for cover but Davies-Scourfield was wounded slightly in the right shoulder blade. When they dusted themselves off they made their way back to their platoons.

At around 10.15 am a vicious struggle developed at Pont Freycinet and Pont Richelieu. From behind the burned out trucks and the smouldering piles of rubble which had been elegant waterfront residences along the Quai de l'Escaut and the Quai de la Tamise, the men of 2KRRC fired at the oncoming Germans. At the barricade on the corner of Rue Edison Captain Claude Bower of 'D' Company was firing a Bren gun from underneath a truck when he fell, wounded under a continuous stream of machine gun fire. Concentrating all their fire on the barricade the Germans were intent on pushing through and the fusilade made it impossible for stretcher bearers to rush out across the street to rescue Captain Bower. Amid the torrent of bullets Riflemen Matthews suddenly careered across the open street in a truck and backed it up to where the stricken officer lay. Jumping out Matthews found Captain Bower already dead and covered with a gas cape, but he removed several other badly wounded riflemen and then made his escape unscathed. For this feat of heroism Rifleman Matthews was awarded the Distinguished Conduct Medal.

Rifleman Eric Chambers, also of 'D' Company, was in a hotel overlooking the bridge area and with a direct view of the Hôtel de Ville and the railway station on the other side of Pont Freycinet. He witnessed a most extraordinary scene as he fired at snipers hiding in the chimney pots of houses on the opposite bank. After the death of Captain Bower the firing at the barricade had stopped and the Germans began to cross the bridge but suddenly, from beneath one of the trucks, Bower's Bren burst into life, firing again and hitting several Germans. It was a bizarre experience and Eric Chambers surmised that Captain Bower's finger had begun to tighten on the Bren's trigger in death.

Dead British soldiers at a barricade.

It was now the turn of the 60th to be squeezed north-eastward in the teeth of the German advance. After the death of Bower at the corner of Rue Edison, the barricades eventually became untenable. German tanks now pushed across Pont Freycinet and fired point blank at the defenders in the ruined houses. German infantry of 1 Battalion 86 Rifle Regiment which followed the tanks across were already swarming into the Rue Jean de Vienne and the Rue Française and were firing on the right flank of Lord Godfrey Cromwell's 'D' Company as they fought their way towards the Citadel. Lord Cromwell was hit by three bullets in both arms and the head as he fired a Bren gun at his barricade in the Place Richelieu, but he stayed at his post until 11.30 am when all but two of his riflemen had been killed and he was compelled to withdraw. The British were fighting for their lives and at his command post in the Theatre Von Oberst Fischer knew it.

Eric Chambers

'Initial successes are reported, further immediate exploitation is ordered. But soon at our observation post we hear increasing MG and rifle fire, the enemy has recovered, he fights for being or not being. Some storm troops have intruded into the Citadel, they were repelled by English counter-attack almost to their starting positions. At the southern border of the city nearly all enemy MG's are operating again, they block the crossing of the canal. Brave and stout hearted officers, corporals and men who try to cross are shot down. The same situation is seen on the right column in the town. The flanking battalion advances but even with heavy fighting it only gains ground slowly. On the left flank the IInd battalion of the Rifle Regiment too is nailed to the ground by the defending fire from the bastion. (Bastion 11) In the command post the mood is rather depressive; the brigadier and the artillery commander remain optimistic... soon it becomes apparent that casualties are low but that the failure of the attack has depressed spirits. Therefore command has to keep spirits up. Based on a new appraisal of the situation... a new concentrated artillery blow immediately followed by a repetition of the attack is ordered.'

Lieutenant Colonel Miller decided to remove his remaining men in stages to make his last stand at a string of posts which stretched across the north-east corner of Calais-Nord: from the Boulevard des Alliés near the Ponts Henri Hénon up along the Rue Nôtre Dame towards 'B' Company positions near the Place d'Angleterre. 'C' Company withdrew along the coast road from their positions along the seafront north of the Citadel to take up a line from Fort Risban to the north-east corner of the Place

The corner of Rue Edison.

d'Armes. They were covered by Captain Radcliffe and his mixed party of eighty riflemen and French volunteers at Bastion 11 who kept the Germans 'nailed to the ground' until they had used up all their ammunition and were completely surrounded, thus enabling the rest of 'C' Company to withdraw. 'B' Company, however, did not fall back into line as Miller had intended due to the fierce battle which had developed along the quays. Lieutenant Colonel Miller and 2/Lieutenant Dick Scott who was at battalion HQ, set out together along the Rue Notre Dame from Place d'Armes to investigate and turned onto the Rue Maréchaux where they became separated. Scott continued in the direction of Major Poole's HQ with the CO's latest orders.

In a house close to the bridge near Place de Norvège an increasingly anxious Major Poole was contemplating his next move now that touch had been lost with the left flank of 'D' Company due to their withdrawal. His casualties were mounting and he was trying to reorganize his line with the help of a platoon of 'C' Company 1QVR under 2/Lieutenant FB Banbury. 2/Lieutenant Davies-Scourfield was returning to Company HQ after visiting the front line to support Sergeant Wall's section in a house on the corner of Rue Hollande and Place de Norvège, a position which was under heavy attack from across the canal. Snipers were still active in the vicinity and as Davies-Scourfield slithered into the cellar of the house being used as HQ he fancied he had been shot at.

'Jack told me later that he himself had been under fire at that spot... Then I saw Dick (Scott): he was crossing the street towards us and smiling cheerfully. He had news for Jack, he shouted ,"Run quickly," I shouted back, "You're under fire." He ran towards the cellar opening, and I grabbed him to pull him in. The bullet went right through his head as I held him. He did not die at once, but he never regained consciousness, lying still and peaceful till he had gone. For a moment I was overcome with anguish, but the battle had to go on.'

With the withdrawal of 1RB and 'D' Company of 2KRRC to their left and right respectively, 'B' Company were in danger of becoming encircled. At around 3pm, Very lights were fired from the Cellulose Factory, a large building set back from the Quai de la Loire and known to many riflemen as the 'brewery', signalling the final onslaught, and German infantry swarmed over the quays and platforms of the Gare Maritime. The Germans pushed 1 Battalion of 69 Rifle Regiment against 1RB whilst the men of 2 Battalion 69 Rifle Regiment fought their way across the bridge near Place de Norvège and worked around the left flank of 'B' Company 2KRRC. The German commanders were delighted by the early promise of the afternoon's assault.

'The exhausted storm troops gather new energy and...having begun a new attack they soon gain ground. Already the initial results are better than those in the morning and it can be reported to the division that according to the brigade Calais shall still fall this day. The attack of the IInd Battalion against the bastion, too, has good results...The second breach in the enemy's defence, perhaps the decisive one, has been made. The capture of the bastion does not fail to have an effect on the Citadel, here too, the enemy begins to grow weaker...But the definite success still fails to appear. The order of the Brigade is "Attack, capture of the Citadel, and destruction of the enemy!" The IInd Battalion advances to Fort Risban and occupies it after some time and supports from the north the fight for the Citadel. The right assault group advances along the eastern border of the city arriving at the southern and southwestern shore of the Bassin des Chasses. The Englishmen stubbornly defend the locks. At the same time the IInd Battalion (of 69 Rifle Regiment) intrudes from the south into the eastern part of the city and engages the English in the north-eastern quarter who are attacking parts of Ist Battalion. The main part of the left assault group now storms from the south and from the east into the Citadel.'

By 3.30 pm 1RB had used up all its ammunition and reserves and had bitten deeply into the 20,000 rounds landed by the Royal Navy a few days earlier. The situation was now critical and they had been forced back to the mound on top of Bastion 1 and among the dunes and trenches east of the Bastion L'Estran, an area no bigger than two football pitches. In the Regimental Aid Post in the tunnel beneath Bastion 1 lay the wounded and

131

the dying, packed like sardines into the dark and filthy recesses of the casemates while the battle raged around and above them. The end was not long in coming. A little after 3.30 pm German infantry of 1 Battalion 69 Rifle Regiment, having forced Major Brush out of his trenches near the Bastion de l'Estran, had surrounded the remnants of 1RB on the top of Bastion 1. The excited voices of the German troops entering the tunnel and the clatter of weapons dropping to the floor signalled the end. Rifleman Don Gurr, arguably the best rifle shot in the British Army at the time, was with Brush's party and fought on until a ricochet went through his left leg just above his ankle and he was taken prisoner. His leg was amputated that night in Calais by a French surgeon but he never understood why he had to lose the whole of his left leg for a wound above the ankle.

Not far away, in the dunes near the beach to the north-east, Rifleman Sam Kydd of 1QVR was hastily digging a slit trench under the orders of his platoon commander 2/Lieutenant Field-Fisher, known affectionately to the men as 'Fee-Fee', after a hazardous retirement some hours earlier.

'The Germans had taken most of the town except for a large pocket of

Scene of destruction at the Gare Maritime.

resistance in and around the harbour - this side of the level crossing.... I was on the beach near a jetty along with three other riflemen and our officer from 'D' Company. For some unaccountable reason we were digging this slit trench when I suddenly spotted some German soldiers away to our right advancing along the beach. I warned 'Fee Fee.' "Right," he said. "In the trench everybody. Move."

It was about three foot deep you couldn't even squat in it - comfortably. To our horror a similar squad of Germans were spotted coming from the opposite direction. We looked at 'Fee Fee' and all he said was "Oh Christ."

He took out his white handkerchief, waved it and turned to us and said, "Sorry, fellows - it's bloody hopeless."

We were soon surrounded by thirty or forty...They were bellowing and motioning with their machine guns and the awful thing was you didn't understand a word they were saying and they in turn took it for dumb insolence. Our rifles and ammo were thrown into the sea and we were searched for any other form of weapon.'

As the men were being searched a German officer arrived, sporting two British revolvers in his belt and a pair of binoculars hung around his neck. He took the opportunity to address his captives with the words, 'for you the war is over'. Glancing north, rifleman Kydd looked wistfully out to sea and was sure that he could see the faint outline of the English coast just twenty-two miles away. He and others, were not to see it again for more than five years.

The *coup de grâce* was delivered an hour later at the Citadel. With the crossing of Pont Freycinet and the infiltration of the streets surrounding Nicholson's HQ the Germans began to take the upper hand. Panzers had surrounded the Citadel by 3 pm and half an hour later the first of the German infantrymen had battered down the Boulogne Gate and were fighting hard along the ramparts.

Colonel Holland told Lieutenant Evitts to walk out of the Citadel and take the first ten men with him. He did so and led the men in single file towards the inner archway of the Boulogne Gate with their hands on their heads.

'A few yards away a small group of German soldiers led by a Feldwebel was coming towards us and others in twos and threes were following up behind. The Feldwebel carried a revolver in his hand and a few grenades in his jack boots... and he looked at me with a face full of scorn and hatred as if he would rather put a bullet through me than look at me.'

The time was 4.30pm and the Citadel had finally fallen.

A short while later Fort Risban was finally overwhelmed and what was left of the units of 2KRRC and 1QVR were fought to a standstill in the Place d'Angleterre and the Place de l'Europe opposite the Pont Vétillard swing bridge. Corporal Ron Savage had been in a house in a prime position with

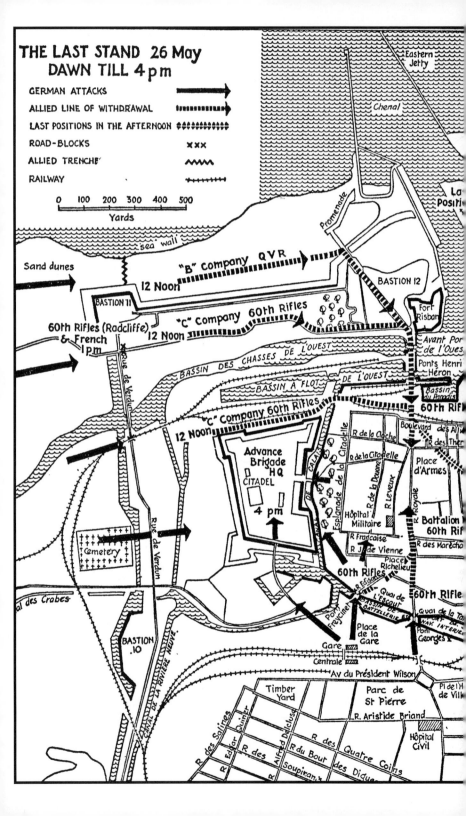

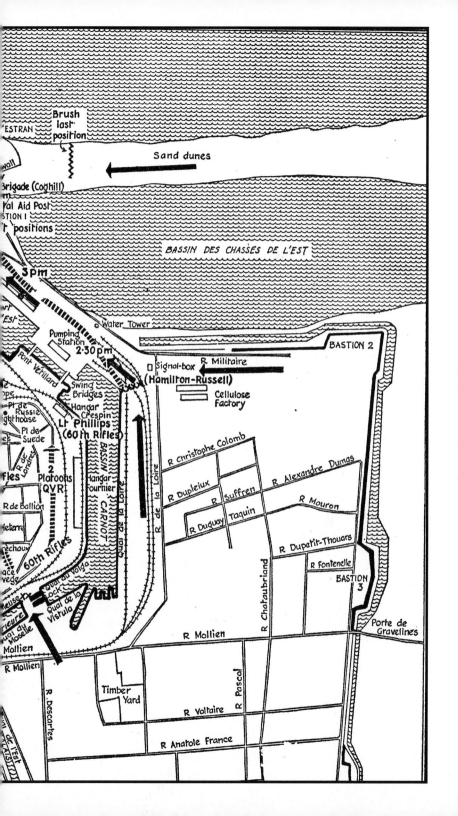

six other riflemen near the Place de Norvège and it was clear they were being surrounded. He decided they would make a break for it.

'One man ran out and got about twenty yards when he let out a holler and dropped. We tried to get down the cellar but we were shot at there so the only way to go was up. We broke through the roof and made our way across the roofs of a row of tenement buildings until we got to the last one. One of the men asked what we were going to do now. I said we had to go down the drainpipe. I slid down so fast it burnt holes in the knees of my trousers but one of the lads passed me on the way down, he fell off! We all got down and made a dash down the street under fire towards the square but as we sheltered in a doorway with bullets splitting the door frame inches from my face one German tank came into the square from the right and another came from the left and they pointed their machine guns at us. There was nothing we could do, we were surrounded.'

A little further north, on a corner of the Quai Paul Devot on the western side of the harbour, Rifleman Thomas Sandford and a small band of his comrades of 'A' Company, 2KRRC prepared to make their last stand 'stubbornly' defending the lock gates. Surrounded on three sides by German soldiers Rifleman Sandford knew there was no escape. Tired beyond belief, without food or water, Sandford and the small band fought on against the relentless probing of the German troops until their last round of ammunition had been used. When the last round had been fired

After the battle the detritus of war litters the quay in front of the Gare Maritime. Note the Pont Vétillard swing bridge and the smashed lock gate of the Écluse Carnot allowing the water through.

Hanger Crespin
See page 184

they sheltered behind what cover they could find and awaited the inevitable. The Germans closed in on the group and a stick grenade was hurled in their direction, exploding a few yards from them. It blew the riflemen off their feet killing some and wounding several others. Dazed and deafened by the blast but otherwise unwounded, Rifleman Sandford struggled to his feet to find the barrel of a German rifle pointed at his chest. Sandford began to take his equipment off and in his dazed and confused state he fumbled with the knot which held his respirator to his chest. To Sandford's horror a German officer drew a knife and approached him. Reaching out he cut at the troublesome cord and removed the respirator. He looked straight at Sandford and in perfect English he said, 'Why do you fight us? You are very brave, but foolish.'

At 4 pm half an hour before the fall of the Citadel, Lieutenant Colonel Miller, no longer in contact with Brigadier Nicholson and realizing that further resistance would only add to his casualties, had issued his final orders for the remnants of the battalion '...to disperse and make their way out of Calais in small parties,' It was now every man for himself. In 'B' Company 2KRRC sector 2/Lieutenant Davies -Scourfield was unaware of any such order. All he knew was that the Germans were now on his right and behind him and he determined to set out and rally the remaining posts of his platoon and to make contact with other platoons to prevent any further German advance into his area. With Germans all around him and under constant fire he ducked and dived between houses and over garden fences.

' I could not, amid all the excitement, remember their exact positions and, while standing near the canal and looking about, I came under fire from across the canal and was hit. I must have been an easy target. One bullet went through my right arm and another hit me in the side. People do not often describe what it feels like to be shot, so I will record that it felt as if I had been clouted in the ribs with a sledgehammer... I staggered a few steps towards a burnt-out truck... but I was hit again , this time in the head. I was conscious of starting to fall and then I must have passed out. When I regained my senses... I found the slightest movement agonizing... My tin hat was still under my head and half full of blood.'

As it grew dark he crawled into a small hut a few yards away and was discovered by chance by a lone German soldier who dressed his wounds with a field dressing and informed him help would come, which it did as dawn broke on 27 May. For 2/Lieutenant Davies-Scourfield the unbelievable had happened and it was with a feeling of shock and dismay that he realized he was now a prisoner of war.

In the Citadel the Germans marshalled the Allied prisoners onto the open space in the central courtyard and set up two machine guns which they trained on the Allied troops. Colonel Holland managed to retrieve his blanket from his batman, Private Weaver of the 7th Worcesters, and shortly afterward he and Brigadier Nicholson were separated from the rest of the dispirited throng and were marched off towards Calais St.Pierre and the German HQ in the Theatre in the Place Albert 1er to be interviewed by Von Oberst Fischer and his officers. As in the cases of Sandford and Kydd, German officers were keen to comment as the two senior British officers passed by.

'On the way a German officer, who passed us said to Brigadier Nicholson in French: "Vous avez battu très courageusement." The same sentiments were repeated at the German Regimental HQ. Here, also, a German officer expressed surprise that we had no artillery. We were allowed to try and retrieve kit, which we had abandoned, when hurriedly evacuating our HQ at the Clinique on 24th. We were driven off together in a car to Desvres. After a halt there we were driven on, and late in the evening reached Montreuil. We could not but remember that this was GHQ in the Great War.' PRO WO217/2

Von Oberst Fischer recorded his feelings at the moment of victory.

'At 17.30 city, Citadel and harbour entrance in our hands. High spirits in this moment dominate in the command posts in the Theatre. Proudly we think of our brave stormtroopers... It was a hot bitter struggle to take this fortress, England's entrance to France. Even the unexpected obstinate defence of the Englishman proves to us that he knew the worth of Calais in all its importance, and therefore the loss of the town must be more grievously felt. Shortly afterwards we hear in the Supreme Command's report the laconic statement "Calais captured." Of the hard struggles which preceded the fall came nothing which could be known at home. Tenaciously the fort had been defended-even more tenaciously our Rifle Regiments had fought... determined to gain their end. So many heroes after the hard fight are now covered with cool earth... Beside Sedan and Somme now Calais too, was entered on the division's page of glory. Sure of victory it looked forward to new tasks.'

As the daylight faded on the remains of Calais that late May evening an eerie silence reigned. At the barricades of Pont Freycinet, Pont Richelieu and Pont Faidherbe; on the street corners near Rue Edison and the Place de Norvège the British and German dead lay slumped amongst the smoking wreckage. Along the ramparts and in the bastions British and French defenders lay side by side where they had fallen during the desperate resistance. The fierce glow from hundreds of burning buildings and vehicles from the Citadel to the old, narrow laned fisherman's quarter known as the 'Courgain', was reflected in the weary eyes of men like Sandford and Kydd as long columns of Allied prisoners of war were marched off to spend long years in captivity. Some of them, Brigadier Nicholson included, would not survive that ordeal. At the same time,

Inside the Citadel after its capture.

thirty six kilometres to the east at Dunkirk, 'Operation Dynamo' began in earnest thus saving 330,000 Allied troops from a similar fate.

The debate as to whether the defence of Calais actually contributed to the 'miracle' of Dunkirk or not has a long history but whatever view is espoused several inescapable facts will always remain. It is a fact that an entire Panzer Division, albeit under strength, was held at Calais for the best part of three days. Whatever the German Command's plans were for the use of its divisions in the assault on Dunkirk it is also a fact that 10 Panzer Division could not be used between 24 and 26 May for any other purpose. If the battle for Calais had not been fought it is a fact that the men, the tanks and the artillery would have been free to have been used elsewhere. It is also a fact that for every hour the Dunkirk perimeter was kept intact it added greatly to the eventual success of the evacuation.

As morning broke over the charred bones of Calais on May 27 the Germans holding the Citadel were astonished to see several RAF Lysanders fly over and drop supplies.

> 'The enemy has not even recognized the loss of the place so important for him; in the morning hours English aeroplanes rush in and drop considerable amounts of ammunition and food on the Citadel having no idea what a pleasant surprise they give to the German combatants by sending them a savoury breakfast!'

And what of the human cost? For the people of Calais their town, particularly the Old-Town, had quite literally disappeared. They lost almost everything and would not begin to rebuild until after the liberation in September 1944. From a military perspective due almost entirely to the nature of the battle and the fact that all the survivors who were left alive were taken prisoner, it has been difficult to ascertain the precise number of British casualties sustained in the fighting. The figures for wounded will never be known as many 'walking' wounded men were treated as able-bodied prisoners as they were marched away and were never officially listed as 'wounded'. The exact figure of those killed in action is also difficult to resolve. The CWGC records the names of 192 men of 1RB, 2KRRC and 1QVR as killed in action or died of wounds received at Calais. It is estimated that a further 100 were lost from 3RTR and the Royal Artillery Anti-Aircraft, Anti-Tank and Searchlights units involved.

Forty seven men jumped on to the Royal Navy yacht *Gulzar* from the wooden piles beneath the extremities of the eastern breakwater during the night of 26/27 May whilst the Germans walked above them and a few determined men such as Captain Alick Williams, the Adjutant of 2KRRC and Major Dennis Talbot, Brigadier Nicholson's Brigade Major, slipped away from the prisoners' column as it was marched south and managed to cross the Channel after some hair raising adventures.

Two hundred wounded men were evacuated before Calais fell. 500 of the more seriously wounded were unable to be evacuated or moved. That left around 2,400 able bodied men who were taken prisoner.

Riflemen Charles Green and Roy Archer had both been evacuated at dawn on 25 May with their twice wounded company CO Major John

In a late attempt to re-supply the besieged defenders twelve Lysanders were sent to Calais arriving at dawn 27 May. The town had fallen to the Germans the previous night and three of the slow flying aircraft were brought down. This one crashed on the ramparts of Fort Risban.

An incredibly brave attempt by pilots of the RAF to fly in needed supplies to 30 Brigade. The supplies they delivered went straight to the German victors.

Taylor and Lieutenant Colonel Chandos Hoskyns, aboard a small yacht. Green and Archer were immediately transferred to hospital. A few days later, recovering in his hospital bed in Leatherhead, Surrey, nursing a bullet wound to his upper right arm which he had sustained whilst firing a Bren gun from beneath a truck on May 24, Rifleman Charles Green, was counting his blessings. He was one of the lucky few; a man who had fought in the Battle of Calais and had returned home. A few days after the capture of most of his Rifle Brigade comrades who had not been killed in battle, Charles Green was able to see visitors and to read the newspapers brought into the hospital.

'When I got back I went into hospital in Leatherhead and

Dennis Talbot

141

my mother came to visit. I was sitting up in bed and she said, " I thought you were dead. The telegram said you had serious head injuries." That would have been on the fifth or sixth day back. After I'd been in hospital a bit I picked up the Daily Mirror *and there was a memorial cartoon. There were all these dead lying on top of one another . The caption said, "This is Calais." You were a hero then I can tell you.'*

The Daily Mirror cartoon seen by Charles Green as he lay in hospital. The original caption read 'Their name liveth for evermore'.

British graves just inside the Neptune Gate of the Citadel. 2/Lieutenant Dick Scott and Captain Claude Bower of 2KRRC were buried here.

Prisoners of War – men of 30 Brigade are employed in clearing up some of the damage at Calais.

MAN WHO LED CALAIS HEROES TAKEN

THE hero of the defence of Calais was named yesterday. He is Brigadier Claude Nicholson, who is now a prisoner of war. Brigadier Nicholson, who is forty-one, is described by General Sir Hubert Gough as the "perhaps most brilliant British officer of his standing."

It was Brigadier Nicholson, with 3,000 British and 1,000 French troops who carried out the order, "Hold Calais to the end," and thereby saved the B.E.F.

He spurned the German demand for surrender, and for four days his forces kept back two German armoured divisions while the B.E.F. embarked at Dunkirk for home. Outnumbered, out-gunned, short of food and ammunition, and attacked by stronger and stronger forces, the Calais defenders fought on—till there was silence.

General Sir Hubert Gough, a close friend of Brigadier Nicholson, said yesterday: "Nicholson is the most able and clear-headed soldier of his age that I know.

★

Brigadier Nicholson, heroic leader of Calais defence, now a prisoner of war in Germany.

Aged forty-two, he was a lieutenant in the Lancers in

"He is now a prisoner of war. His wife has had a letter from him since his capture. He was always a 16th Lancer. After going through the Staff College he became one of the senior instructors there and was later given special promotion to command the regiment.

"He took the regiment to India and commanded them for about two years. Just before the war broke out he appointed Commandant of the Imperial Defence College.

Supreme Courage

"Six months after the outbreak of war he was given command of this light brigade which did so magnificently at Calais.

"Nicholson has that greatest of all qualities, courage, in great degree. He is absolutely resolute, both in the face of the enemy and in all his dealings. He is not in the least afraid to say what he thinks.

"None the less he is receptive of modern ideas.

"We had heard from other sources that he had been captured, and now a letter from him to his wife has con-

After the German occupation a lone German motorcyclist pauses to find his way near the monument to the *Sauveteurs* (Lifeboat men) which stood on the Boulevard des Alliés. It is now positioned on the Quai Delpierre.

Last Stand at Calais by Charles Gere RA. It depicts a stylized scene showing Brigadier Nicholson surrounded by his senior officers on the ramparts of the Citadel near the Neptune Gate.

German sniper's eye view of the waterfront and the area around Pont Faidherbe from the clock tower of the Hôtel de Ville.

British prisoners from 30 Brigade and some French prisoners awaiting transport away from Calais.

Above: After the battle. View south from the top of the lighthouse looking down Rue de Madrid towards B Coy 2KRRC positions around the Place d' Angleterre.

Right: The same view today.

a
by
he

ld
he
r-

he
he
ns
ks
rd

N "
im-
lief
ore
han
ian

not
it
eft
sts
ive

Rifleman David Hossington describing his part in the defence of Calais to Colonel Walter Elliot, M.P. (centre) in London yesterday. Others in this News Chronicle picture are (from left to right) Major Alec Williams, Major Denis Talbot and Lance-Corporal Norman Illingworth.

Men From Calais Tell Of Fight Against Odds

By GEOFFREY MURRAY
News Chronicle Reporter

Brigadier C. Nicholson, when he led his 3,000 Londoners to the defence of Calais, had these instructions, "Do what you can."

So his Brigade Major, Denis Talbot, of Tonbridge, Kent, said to the News Chronicle yesterday, when for the first time four of the men who fought at Calais were allowed to tell their own stories.

"We disembarked at Calais 23 and marched to the

Some of the ones who got away.

TOURS BY CAR

TOUR 1
The Outer Perimeter to the West; Bastion 11, Fort Lapin, Oyez Farm and Fort Nieulay. Allow one day

From the tourist office in the **Boulevard Clemenceau** take the **Rue Royale** north until it becomes the **Rue de la Mer** and cross the **Boulevard de la Résistance** at its junction with the **Boulevard des Alliés**. Cross the two bridges known as the **Ponts Henri Hénon** towards **Fort Risban**. Keeping Fort Risban on your right, turn **left** onto the **Boulevard du Général de Gaulle**. Take the **fifth turn** on your right which has a signpost for the 'Aquar'ile Restaurant. This is the **Rue de Maréchal de Juin**. Follow this road and you will see quite clearly a steep and regular grassy slope rising to approximately 15m in height. This earth rampart is all that remains of Bastion 11. Take the **left turn** into the **Rue Jean Moulin** and drive up to the **car park of the 'Les Ridens'** apartment building which stands on top of the site of the Bastion.

It was here that a small mixed force of riflemen of 2KRRC and French soldiers and sailors known as the 'Volunteers of Calais' under the overall command of Captain Everard Radcliffe of 2KRRC, covered the withdrawal of 'C' Company 2KRRC during the afternoon of 26 May. By the time they had been surrounded and captured at around 1 pm that afternoon they had been under attack for some ten hours and the senior French officer Capitaine Michel de la Blanchardière had been wounded severely. Seventeen Frenchmen were captured and fifty out of the eighty riflemen involved were wounded. The way to the Citadel had been opened.

Park the car and walk to the eastern edge of the car park and look back towards Calais Nord. Looking above the rooftops of the houses on the Rue Jean Moulin you can begin to get a German soldier's eye view of the old town of Calais-Nord and Calais St. Pierre and why the capture of Bastion 11 was so important in unlocking the defences of the Old Town. In the gap between the roofs of the present day houses you can see the grassy ramparts of the Citadel. Beyond and to the left you can pick out the spire of Notre Dame and the Tour de Guet in the Place D'Armes. Further still to the left can be seen the derricks of the port much as they would have

Bastion 11. The grassy slopes are all that remain of this outer perimeter defence position. It was here that the French 'Volunteers of Calais' and some eighty riflemen of 2KRRC covered the withdrawal of C Company 2KRRC.

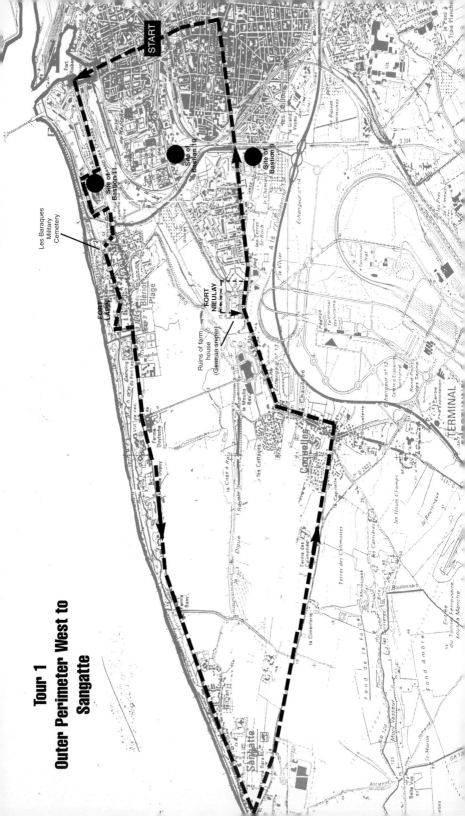

Tour 1
Outer Perimeter West to Sangatte

START

Les Baraques Military Cemetery

Site of Bastion 11

Site of Bastion 10

Site of Bastion 9

FORT LAPIN

Blériot Plage

FORT NIEULAY

Ruins of farm house (German sniper)

Coquelles

Chaussée

TERMINAL

Sangatte

looked in May 1940. Looking to the right the distinctive clock tower of the Hôtel de Ville comes into view.

It was from the position you are standing that, after the capture of Bastion 11, the Germans were able to fire with deadly accuracy on the defenders of Fort Risban, the Citadel and other key points.

From the car park drive downhill and **turn left**, then **left again** into the **Rue du Maréchal Leclerc**.

The area between the site of Bastion 11 and Fort Risban was once the site of a French military barracks and the arsenal was situated on this road. The preponderance of street names honouring French officers also bears testimony to the former use of the area.

Drive around the foot of the Bastion and return to the Boulevard du Général De Gaulle. Just before you reach the road junction note a small road to your right named in honour of Commandant Carlos de Lambertye the French Commander of Calais during the battle. He collapsed and died of a heart attack whilst crossing Ponts Henri Hénon returning to his HQ in Fort Risban after rallying his troops.

Turn **right** onto the Boulevard du Général De Gaulle and travel towards **Blériot Plage,** which, before 1936, was called Les Baraques. After a short distance you will come to a roundabout. Take the **D940** coast road signposted **Sangatte**, then take the **third turn** on the right when you see the distinctive green and white signpost of the Commonwealth War Graves Commission towards **Les Baraques Military Cemetery**. At the next road junction **turn left** onto the **Rue Vigier**. Driving down the road you will see the high brick wall of the local village cemetery to your right. Les Baraques Military Cemetery is a further two hundred metres down the road nestling behind the sand dunes. There is ample parking off the road to your left opposite the entrance to the cemetery.

Two Riflemen, Jack Freeman and William Long lie in the cemetery, which dates from the First World War when Calais was a large British base and hospital centre. The cemetery was in use between September 1917 and 1921 when the last British troops left France and the final total of 1914-18 burials was 1,562. Apart from the two known 2KRRC burials two more soldiers and three airmen of the Second World War are also buried here. The soldiers and one of the airmen are, however, unidentified.

Continue down the Rue Vigier and take the third turn on your right which is the **Rue du Semaphore**. Continue to the end of the road and you will drive onto an area of open land near the dunes. You will also see a tumbledown concrete bunker which was once part of the German coastal defence system.

Turn around and return along the **Rue du Semaphore** then turn **right** at the junction with **Rue Vigier**. Take the **next right turn** which is a continuation of Rue Vigier and follow the road until it turns sharp left. Park the car and walk up into the area of the dunes towards **Fort Lapin**.

The site around Fort Lapin is known as the **Dunes de Fort Mahon** and is now an area of natural beauty, cordoned off in certain areas to prevent further erosion of the sand dunes. Walking up the rise towards Fort Lapin you will first notice a German ferro-concrete bunker ahead of you. As you walk up the hill notice also the damaged concrete and the rusting metal rods at ground level which give some indication of the extent and strength of the German fortifications along the coast in this area. The German fortifications here are the remains of a battery of 164.7mm guns which defended the seafront.

Fort Lapin is sited next to the German fortification and is easily distiguished from

Fort Lapin built by Vauban during the 17th century. The yellow brick construction contrasts with the concrete bunkers built during the German occupation.

the German construction as it was built by the engineers of Vauban in 1690 out of the yellow bricks so typical of the Calais area. The fort is now in ruins with evidence of a major roof fall and due to its dangerous state the public are no longer allowed access to the site; fences and signs quite clearly restrict entry in order to reduce the risk of injury or death. It is still possible, however, to see the nature of its construction and some of the renovation work carried out in the eighteenth century in the years prior to the Franco-Prussian War of 1870. Evidence of this refurbishment can be seen quite clearly above the main entrance where the date 1860 has been worked into the keystone.

At the start of the battle for Calais the garrison of Fort Lapin was part of the French coastal defences under the overall command of **Le Capitaine de Frégate Carlos de Lambertye**. The garrison consisted of 150 French marines under the command of **Lieutenant de Vaisseau Sequier** and the fort's weaponry consisted of

The ruins of Fort Lapin are in a dangerous state (1999). M. Georges Fauquet, my guide to the area.

four 164mm guns, two 37mm guns, one 25mm gun, two 8mm machine guns as well as a 150cm searchlight. Although the heavy and medium coastal guns were designed to fire out to sea and indeed in several defensive positions along the coast around Calais they were practically useless against a land attack, the guns at Fort Lapin were able to be fired on the Germans.

The French gunners were in action towards 3 pm on May 23 when they fired on a column of German armour advancing from the direction of Coquelles (to the south-west). The following day, the 24 May, at 5.30 in the morning they fired on German gun positions near the cliffs of Cap Blanc Nez and then concentrated their fire on the crossroads in Coquelles from where the Germans were signalling, thereby aiding the garrison of Fort Nieulay then under attack from German artillery. When the gunners ran out of ammunition orders were given to spike the guns so as to render them useless to the Germans in case of capture.

From the parking area near the fort drive down the **Rue du Fort Lapin** for a short distance until you reach the junction with the **D 940** which is the main road to Sangatte. **Turn right** and drive past some industrial units on your left until you come to a roundabout, easily recognizable as it has a small fishing boat 'beached' in the centre of it. Go straight across towards Sangatte and drive past a signpost bearing the words **Les Salines**. Pull in here and park the car carefully as there is not much by way of a verge at this point and look across the open country to your left. Note the ridge of high ground running roughly north-west from the cliffs at Cap Blanc Nez to the south-east, including the village of Coquelles. The Germans held this ridge of high ground from dawn on 24 May and it is evident that it gave them an enormous advantage over the defenders in terms of providing superior observation and gun placement for their artillery.

Drive on and after approximately 800 metres you will come to a group of farm buildings on your left known as **Ferme Dupuy** on the IGN 1:25 000 map of Calais. Parking is possible with care on the raised verge on your right. This farm was better known to the British troops as **Oyez Farm** in May 1940. It was particularly well known to the men of 'B' Company, 1QVR under the command of Captain G.P. Bowring and gunners of the 6th Heavy Anti- Aircraft Battery Royal Artillery.

The British guns were sited in the dunes to your right and to the rear of the farm and it was here that they were joined on the night of 23 May by Captain Bowring and his men, whose allotted task on disembarkation was an unenviable march of six and a half kilometres, carrying all their equipment and ammunition on foot to block the coast road west to Boulogne at this point and to patrol the shoreline for a distance of three miles. From this point 2/ Lieutenant Freddy Nelson led Rifleman Edward Lyme and the rest of 6 platoon of 'B' Company, 1QVR across country to join Captain Tim Munby at a road block on the Coquelles road prior to them all joining the French garrison inside Fort Nieulay on the evening of 23 May.One plane was destroyed on the night of 21 May and the following night a reporter from the BBC claimed on the air that he had seen the British AA battery shoot down a German plane.

'Oyez Farm' today is owned by M. and Mme. Dupuy and run by their son. Mme. Dupuy remembers British troops setting up their guns in the sand dunes on the opposite side of the road from the farm. M. Dupuy was in the French Army in 1940 and was captured near Boulogne as the Germans advanced up the coast. He was marched first to Germany where he was put to work building Autobahns and was then placed in a POW camp in Poland.

The Germans also made use of this site to construct an anti- aircraft battery after

Ferme Dupuy, better known to the territorials of 1 QVR and the gunners of 6 Heavy Anti-Aircraft Battery as Oyez Farm.

the occupation. The battery consisted of four 88mm flak guns and was one of the principal batteries of the schwere Flak Abteilung 501, each armed with 88mm guns. The others were sited at Ferme Trouille, (six guns), now known as Ferme Duytsche on the modern map, Bastion 12, (four guns), and a further six guns in the Petit Courgain area to the east of the Pont de Gravelines

Continue along the **D940** towards Sangatte noting in the open fields to your left the isolated concrete bunkers which were built during the German occupation. 5 Platoon of 'B' Company 1 QVR under 2/Lieutenant J M Dizer were sent forward a further one and a half kilometres from Oyez Farm after the deployment of the rest of 'B' Company at 11 pm on the night of 23 May. Their allotted task was to guard the terminal for the submarine cable link to England and destroy it if there was a risk of its capture by the advancing Germans. As you enter Sangatte reflect on the advanced position and the isolation felt by the men of this platoon of proud Territorial soldiers who had been pitched straight into action with little forward planning, precious little equipment and little training for the role they were being asked to perform.

Drive through the main street of **Sangatte**. A little further along the road **turn left immediately after the church** onto the **D 243 E** signposted, 'A16 (Calais), Coquelles, Guines' and 'Autres Directions'. This road follows the lower slopes of the ridge of high ground which overlooks the flat land north – east towards the coast and Calais itself. After approximately one kilometre notice a German blockhouse to your right now being used as storage by a local farmer. Drive past *La Cimenterie* on your right and after another kilometre take a **left turn** where the road forks and drive into the village of **Coquelles**.

It was from their assembly area around Coquelles that Lieutenant Colonel Reginald Keller, commanding officer of 3RTR advanced south at 2.15 p.m. and forty-five minutes later engaged a strong enemy column of the 1st Panzer Division moving north – east near Hames Boucres just north of Guines.

At the crossroads in the **centre of Coquelles turn left** and drive towards Calais. It was from this position that the Germans were observed signalling on 24 May by the French troops in Fort Lapin and as a result the French naval guns of the fort

154

concentrated their fire on the area. You are now following the route of the German armour as it made its way **towards Fort Nieulay** during the afternoon of 24 May. The German command post during the battle for Fort Nieulay was in a small wood to the right of the main road just before the road begins to bend to the right. It was from this wood that the German infantry first appeared in order to assault the fort.

Drive on until you come to a **roundabout** close to the **Auchan** hypermarket. Sainsbury's also has a store close by. Go **straight across** the roundabout towards Calais on the **N1, Avenue Roger Salengro** and very soon you will see the imposing brick curtain walls of Fort Nieulay come into view on your left. **Turn left** into the car park which is set back off the road over a small bridge. Take care to make sure the road is clear before making the turn as the oncoming traffic tends to travel with great speed towards Coquelles and Boulogne along this stretch of straight road. At this point you are only about one and a half kilometres west of the Pont Jourdan bridge and some five and a half kilometres from the ferry port. **Fort Nieulay** is an impressive testimonial to the genius of that great French military engineer Sébastien Le Prestre de Vauban. It has undergone a dramatic transformation during the last decade and is now open to the general public. It was something of a dream of M. Georges Fauquet, a prominent member of the Calais historical society, that the fort, which had fallen into a lamentable state of disrepair over the years, be renovated. It was eventually purchased by the town of Calais, supported by National government funding and after several years of hard work by many dedicated people it now appears that the dream of M. Fauquet is becoming reality. The commanding officer's quarters, the guard room of the eastern gate and the south-west Bastion have undergone dramatic yet sympathetic transformations, but the *pièce de résistance* is the completely renovated 'powder room' which now houses a small, but very absorbing exhibition of the history of the fort from its earliest beginnings.

The origins of the strategic importance of Fort Nieulay as an advanced defensive position for the town of Calais, go back hundreds of years but the most impressive phase of development in Fort Nieulay's history began in 1677. It is the legacy of that development under the direction of Vauban, which we can still see today. The construction of Nieulay on its present site took three years and the work was almost entirely built on piles due to the marshy nature of the ground. Vauban was convinced that Fort Nieulay was the key to the defence of Calais and considered it the ultimate means of resistance to be able to flood the surrounding area when threatened with an invading force. Nieulay's combination of fortifications and integral sluices is unique in this type of construction.

It is possible to see other evidence of later military development in the fields surrounding the fort. Between 1692 and 1700 the western defences were reinforced with the addition of a 'horn' shaped construction. During the same period the Commander of Calais, Iries De Laubanie, built an embankment linking Fort Nieulay to the Citadel in Calais Nord and sited several redoubts along its course.

From the end of the C18 the story of Fort Nieulay is one of declining fortunes. With the downgrading of Calais as a key site of defence, Fort Nieulay was shorn of its strategic value and it was subject to severe neglect. Gradually, as the elements took over, the earth banks crumbled and infilled the trenches, the door arches and bridges gave way and the locks ceased to function. By 1870 the fort had been virtually abandoned by the French Army and an air of ruin descended on it as the barracks and the officers' quarters fell down brick by brick. In 1903 the army finally sold the fort for 42,000 francs.

Fort Nieulay. The eastern entrance, otherwise known as the Porte Royale. through the gate at the far side of the fort Porte Dauphine can be clearly seen.

Today Vauban's fort is an impressive sight as you see it for the first time approaching from the Boulogne Road. From the car park you will first see a gate in the south wall. The two main entrances, however, are the Porte Dauphine to the west and the Porte Royale to the east. Follow the path to your right and walk around the outside of the walls until you come to the Porte Royale or Calais gate. Once inside take time to look into the gate house which has a selection of very interesting free leaflets on the history of Nieulay and the fortified towns trail. In the inner courtyard notice the elaborate system of locks and sluices which are now dry. The canal which the locks controlled ran from north to south. Looking to the east one can see the officers' quarters and to the west of the locks the façade of a chapel built around 1690. The chapel served as a parish church; its registers are still kept in the Hôtel de Ville, and had its own burial ground. In August 1999 I was allowed access to the German concrete bunker built in the north-east corner and was amazed to find, laid out on the floor in the gloom, the remains of at least nine human skeletons which had been unearthed during the recent renovations. The rebuilt powder room is situated towards the north-west corner. Further extensive excavations and renovations have been carried out under the south-west bastion. It is possible to walk into the tunnel under the bastion and to see the features which have been uncovered such as the oven along the left hand wall which would have been used to bake bread for the garrison. Coming out of the bastion walk up onto the top of the ramparts for an excellent view of the surrounding countryside.

Standing atop the western ramparts and bastions gazing south-west, one can get a very good idea, (if one allows the eye to dismiss the new building of the commercial zone in the near distance), of the view of Captain A N L Munby's small, mixed force of fifty men of 1QVR and three from 1 Searchlight Regiment as they stood to, peering out into the half – light of dawn on Friday 24 May, with the garrison of forty French troops under Capitaine Herremann. Positioned along the ramparts and in the two western bastions they sought shelter from the German bombardment which began at 5.00 am and then watched anxiously as German infantry of 86 Rifle Regiment emerged from the wood near Coquelles to attack the fort. From this lofty position the advantages offered to the Germans by their domination of the high ground to the west and south-west become obvious. That initial attack was repulsed but repeated assaults on the small force inside Nieulay went on all day. A very heavy bombardment at 2 o'clock in the afternoon was the prelude to another attack which was launched at 2.45 p.m. when tanks advanced from Coquelles. Shells from the Panzers and from the artillery on the high ground began to smash into the brick curtain walls and rained down onto the glacis in front of them. Many shells fell inside the fort itself. Sergeant Ernie Osborne fired his Bren gun from the top of the north-

Above: **Interior of Fort Nieulay. The refurbished guard room at the eastern gate.**

Right: **Remains of the locks and sluices.**

west bastion and pulled the barrel off with the help of Rifleman Edward Lyme. Along these ramparts Corporal John Dexter witnessed the death of Rifleman Leslie Jakob, news of which would not reach Jakob's family for thirty years when information sent by Dexter from Pow camp in 1941 was 'discovered' at QVR HQ in London. Note the concrete emplacement on top of the British position erected by the Germans after the occupation.

By half past three on the afternoon of 24 May, the German artillery fire had reached a crescendo and with German troops advancing to within one hundred yards of the walls under cover of a concentrated mortar barrage, Capitaine Herremann reached the conclusion that the force could no longer hold out. The fort was surrendered and by 4.30 pm the Swastika had been run up the flagpole signalling its capture. In September 1944 the roles of defender and assailant were reversed as the Germans tried to hold off the Allied attacks by organizing a defence of Fort Nieulay. The defence was broken by Canadian troops of the Royal Winnipeg Rifles supported by 'Crocodiles' – tanks fitted with flame

View towards the coast road from the north west bastion.

View riflemen of 1QVR had from the north west bastion as they observed the progress of elements of the German 86 Rifle Regiment.

throwers – on 27 September, 1944. The marks of machine-gun bullets on the concrete blockhouse and the scorching of some of the walls are reminders of the struggle to liberate Nieulay on that day. A plaque on the wall just inside the gate in the south wall commemorates this action and there is talk of turning the German blockhouse into some form of museum.

It is well worth while taking a walk along the path around the outer perimeter of

Entrance to tunnels under the bastion where wounded QVR men were sheltered.

The view outside the fort from the position held by german snipers.

the fort to get a feel of the size of the place. Walk around to the West Gate and then turn west to walk across the grass until you come to a small bridge. Cross the bridge and enter the scrub land via a path. To your right and left approximately 400 metres from the walls of Fort Nieulay, you will see the ruins of brick-built farm buildings. In 1940 the farm buildings were still intact and German snipers took up positions in them to harry the defenders. It is possible to push through the bushes to the ruins on your left and, with great care, stand on them to look back at the fort to get the view the German snipers had. Please do exercise caution here. As with any old building it can be unsafe and I would certainly not recommend it for those who have difficulties with mobility. Walk back around the southern wall of the fort back to the car park.

Turn left out of the car park and drive towards Calais along the Avenue Roger Salengro. This avenue is a long, straight and usually busy road which terminates at a roundabout. Drive **straight across** the roundabout and take the **first right after the bridge** over the Canal de la Rivière Neuve, into the **Quai Catinat** where it is much less busy and **parking** is available.

You are now in the heart of the positions taken up by 'B' Company 2KRRC during the night of 23 May. **Walk north** towards the **Boulevard Léon Gambetta**. Major Jack Poole set up his HQ in the building almost directly opposite the abattoir, which is marked on his original sketch map, and can be seen on your left. **Turn left** and walk towards the roundabout until you come to the bridge over the canal marked on the map as Pont Jourdan. On the opposite bank to the south of the main road is the **Stade Geo André** which now stands on the site of Bastion 9. It was here that 2/Lieutenant Davies-Scourfield deployed the men of his scout platoon and endured the German attacks of 24 May with tanks and infantry pushing hard against the canal and railway bridges. By 8 pm that evening the Germans were just two hundred metres beyond Bastion 9. It was from this position that a patrol of three scout carriers led by 2/Lieutenant Dick Scott drove towards Coquelles past Fort Nieulay early in the morning of 24 May and ran into the advancing Germans. One lone carrier returned to Company HQ to report the loss of the rest of Scott's patrol and 2/Lieutenant Scott himself arrived back at 9.30 am after escaping from the

Bridge over the Canal de la Rivière Neuve, near the site of Bastion 9, marked on present-day maps as 'Pont Jourdan'.

Pont Jourdan railway bridge, looking towards the canal and the site of Bastion 9. Note the building on the right – site of B Coy 2KRRC HQ 23/24 May 1940. The building on the left is the Abattoir.
Inset: The Abattoir (refer to sketch map on page 62 marked as the 'Slaughter House'.

Germans and walking all the way from Fort Nieulay. It was also on this bridge that 2/Lieutenant Davies Scourfield met Major Oswald 'Puffin' Owen at around 4.30 am on the morning of 25 May during the battle for the outer perimeter at the Pont Jourdan leaning against the rail. He told Davies-Scourfield not to continue with his mission to patrol beyond Bastion 9 thus preventing him from running into strong German forces. Davies-Scourfield turned back leaving Puffin Owen on the bridge with his camel stick under his arm as if 'he had no care in the world'. He never saw him again.

Cross the road and **walk back along the Boulevard Léon Gambetta** to the bridge over the railway. This bridge is now known as Pont Gambetta but in 1940 it was this bridge which was known to all who fought in the area as the Pont Jourdan railway bridge. Note how the road falls a little and runs straight towards the centre of Calais St.Pierre and reflect on why it was so vital to prevent a German breakthrough at this point. Lieutenant Airey Neave was sent up to fight in this area and it was on the railway line below you that he met Major Jack Poole who ordered Neave to get his men into houses on either side of the bridge and 'fight like bloody hell'.

Return to the car. At this point you can either take the Boulevard Léon Gambetta into St. Pierre and then back towards the Old Town or turn left towards the roundabout and take the first right to follow the line of the canal and the outer perimeter along the Rue de Verdun. The former route takes you past a private house on the right hand side at 107 Boulevard Léon Gambetta, which in 1940 was known as the 'Clinique', and which served as the HQ for both Colonel Holland and later Brigadier Nicholson. Lieutenant Austin Evitts slept in the basement here on the night he arrived in Calais to set up wireless communications with Dover. The Boulevard Gambetta terminates at the Place Albert 1er. On the right, with its façade on the Boulevard Pasteur, is the Theatre or the Opera, the fourth floor and roof of which were chosen as the HQ and observation post respectively of 10 Schützen Brigade of 10 Panzer Division, commanded by Von Oberst Fischer, when the Germans moved up into St. Pierre during the night of 24 May. **Turn left** onto the **Boulevard Jacquard** and return to the tourist office passing the Hôtel de Ville on your right and crossing the Pont Georges V.

The latter route via the Rue de Verdun follows the course of the canal and the

The 'Clinique HQ of Colonel Holland and later Brigadier Nicholson.

line of the ramparts which ran in front of it in this section of the outer perimeter until the road sweeps left just before the traffic lights at the Pont de Douaumont. **Turn right** at the traffic lights towards Calais. You are still on the Rue de Verdun at this point. Almost immediately on your right are the buildings of a retirement home which is situated on the site of Bastion 10. This bastion was the left flank of 'C' Company 2 KRRC on 24 May and several road blocks were set up on all the rail and canal bridges in this sector although the line of the main road has changed significantly.

Turn left after some 200 metres into the car park of the **Cimetière Nord**. 'C' Company 2KRRC held the line of the ramparts just to the east of the cemetery and during the attacks of 24 May the Germans worked their way into the cemetery during the afternoon and threatened to break through 'C' Company's line with tanks at the junction with 'B' Company held by 11 platoon under 2/Lieutenant Pat Sherrard. The line was stabilized by the appearance of Sergeant Dryborough Smith's section which brought enfilade fire to bear on the cemetery. The Germans withdrew and the pressure eased.

This municipal cemetery is very interesting as it has a military extension to the rear dating from the First World War. Here the dead of two Allied nations lie together with their German counterparts. In 1940 when the German infantry forced their way into the cemetery they were fighting amongst the tombstones of 394 of their countrymen who were killed between 1914 and 1918, as well as the graves of 1048 French and 1060 Belgian war dead.

Return to the car and turn left out of the car park and then first left again on to the Boulevard du 8 Mai. This road follows almost exactly the line of the old ramparts held by 'C' Company 2KRRC from Bastion 10 to Bastion 11 near the coast. After 500 metres the road bends to the right and a pedestrian track off to the left continues the 2 KRRC line as far as the Boulevard du Général de Gaulle and the site of Bastion 11 where we started the tour. Stay on Boulevard du 8 Mai to **skirt the northern face of the Citadel** until it becomes the Boulevard de la Résistance, **turning right** at the cross roads on to the Rue de la Mer and completing the tour by returning to the tourist office via the **Rue Royale**.

German war graves. The line of trees beyond the Cross of Sacrifice mark the line of the Outer Perimeter held by C Coy, 2KRRC.

TOURS BY CAR

TOUR 2

The Outer Perimeter to the South and East, Coulogne, Orphanage Farm
and Les Attaques. Allow one day

From the tourist office in the **Boulevard Clemenceau** drive south and cross the **Pont Georges V** and the **Pont Jacquard** on to the **Boulevard Jacquard**. At the major junction in the Place Albert 1er drive straight across onto the Boulevard Pasteur until you see the Hôtel de Postes in the Place d'Alsace directly in front of you. A one way system operates in this part of St.Pierre, so take the right fork which is the Rue des Fontinettes. Just before the road reverts to a two-way carriageway, almost opposite the Rue Martyn, is the Station des Fontinettes and it was in this area that Lieutenant Colonel Ellison-MacCartney of 1QVR established his first HQ on the evening of 22 May. Drive on until the **Rue des Fontinettes** becomes the **Rue du Cheval Gris** which terminates in a roundabout. This is the Porte de Lille and on the far side of the roundabout you will see a new building known as the Gymnase. Take the fourth exit up the slope of the Rampe de Valenciennes. This area has witnessed significant development in recent years to accommodate the building of the A16 Autoroute which you see in front of you.

As you climb the slope you are climbing up and over the line of the old ramparts of the outer perimeter and the site of Bastion 8 which had disappeared long before the battle for Calais began to make way for the railways which converge beneath you, thus weakening the defences in this sector. It was for this reason that the platoons of 'D' Company 1QVR were sent out beyond the outer perimeter in this area to block all the main approaches into Calais from the south. It is worth remembering how far you have just driven and to reflect on the fact that 1QVR had to complete the journey on foot carrying all their equipment as they had been stripped of most of their transport. The Autoroute to the left follows the line of the ramparts until it reaches Junction 16 at which point the exit road runs north and follows the old line.

Drive under the Autoroute. The road bends to the left sharply and descends towards buildings. **Take the first right turn** into the Chemin des Regniers which is the **D246** signposted '**Fréthun**'. After a short distance the road leaves the houses and runs parallel to the railway line when it becomes the Route de Fréthun. Continue until you reach the road and rail bridges over the Canal de la Rivière Neuve, where it is possible to park. You will see that this is a relatively new construction and has been resurfaced but in 1940 it was the 'hump back' bridge where Sam Kydd and the men of 11 platoon, QVR set up their first road block in the dip on the Calais side. Although the rail traffic has increased enormously due to the close proximity of the Channel Tunnel freight and passenger terminals less than two kilometres to the west, one can see how easy it was to obtain rail sleepers from the tracks just metres away with which to improve the barricade.

Continue under the road bridge ahead until the road bears left. At the 'Stop' sign take the **D246 E1** signposted 'Calais, Coulogne and Coquelles'. This is the **Route de Nielles. Turn right** onto the **D304** and left at the roundabout on to the **D246 E** towards Coulogne. This becomes the D245 (Rue des Chataigniers.) **Turn**

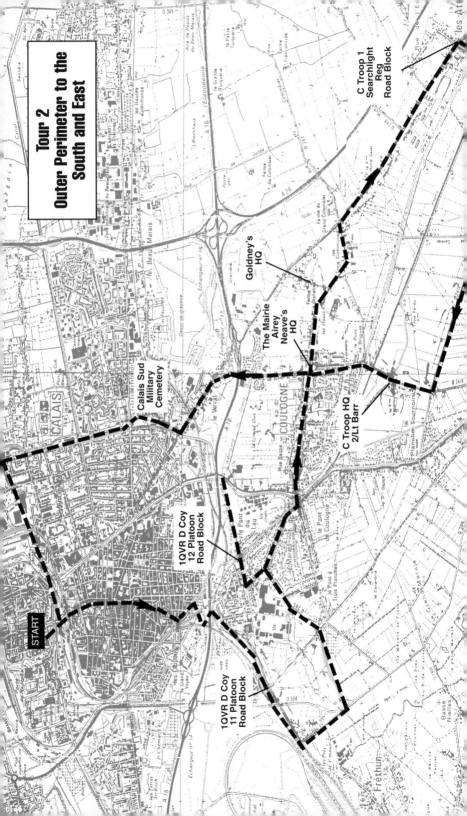

**Tour 2
Outer Perimeter to the
South and East**

C Troop 1
Searchlight
Reg
Road Block

Goldney's HQ

The Mairie
Airey Neave's HQ

Calais Sud
Military
Cemetery

C Troop HQ
2/Lt Barr

CALAIS

COULOGNE

1QVR D Coy
12 Platoon
Road Block

1QVR D Coy
11 Platoon
Road Block

START

Fréthun

Initial positions of D Coy 1 QVR at the site of their roadblock built by 11 Platoon on the route De Fréthun.

left at the give way sign and then take the **third right** into the Rue Montreal. Drive up to the **level crossing and park the car**. Here at the crossroads of the Route de Coulogne and the Chemin de Grand Voyeau directly opposite, was the first position of 12 platoon 1QVR under 2/Lieutenant Brewester blocking the road to Guines. At this point you are some 700 metres beyond the outer perimeter and the site of Bastion 8. The German attack at dawn on 24 May hit these isolated road blocks of the Territorials hardest and 2/Lieutenant Brewester had to withdraw to the line of the ramparts at 7 am. Carefully **cross the railway line** and walk down the Chemin de Grand Voyeau to its junction with the Quai d'Amerique. **Turn left**, passing beneath the Autoroute and after 500 metres you will come to the railway bridge known as Pont de Fer the 'Iron Bridge'. This is the line of withdrawal taken by Brewester, who took up a position on the ramparts just to the right of the bridge in which position his men were fired on from behind by German snipers who had broken through into the Boulevard Curie to your rear right.

Return to the car and drive back along the Rue Montreal, turning left at the junction and follow the road into Coulogne itself, the Chemin des Regniers. **Take the left turn** over the Canal de Calais at the Pont de Coulogne. A short distance after crossing the canal the road forks. **Take the right fork** and follow signs for the Mairie. The fairly narrow road runs through a residential area until it opens out into the cross roads of Coulogne where the road bends to the right and you will see the Mairie directly ahead of you. There is ample **parking in front of the Mairie**. Lieutenant Airey Neave set up his HQ in this building which was built in 1830, and began to organize the defence of Coulogne with his men of 'F' Troop, 2 battery, 1 Searchlight Regiment RA. Notice the long straight road leading south to the Pont des Briques which Neave thought a difficult road to defend. **With your back to the Mairie** walk across the road and take the narrow lane up to the church. Over by the wall to your right as you enter the churchyard you will see the CWGC headstone which marks the grave of Neave's twenty-one year old dispatch rider, Gunner

165

Crossroads in the centre of Coulogne. The Mairie was used by Airey Neave as F Troop HQ, 20 to 23 May 1940.

Reginald Branton, killed in action during the battle for Coulogne on 23 May at the age of 21. To the left of the gate is a memorial to the dead of the Coulogne rail disaster of 15 May 1940, when eighteen French and Belgian war evacuees were killed as their train collided with a goods train from St Omer.

Return to the car and take the **D247** signposted **Les Attaques**. After 800 metres or so you will see a group of red brick and white buildings down a long track to your left. It is possible to **park the car here** and walk down to the buildings known collectively as the Ferme des Orphelins or Orphanage Farm to the British. On 23 May 1940 it was the HQ of Colonel Goldney commanding 1 Searchlight Regiment. During the assault on Les Attaques and Coulogne by 1 Panzer Division on 23 May which commenced at 2pm, Colonel Goldney held the farm with a padre a medical

Orphanage Farm HQ of Colonel Goldney, 1 Searchlight Regiment, during the fight for Les Attaques 23 May.

officer and a few men until 7 pm when shellfire set part of the farm alight and he had to withdraw to the line of the Outer Perimeter. The farm is now private property and part of it is used as a college. Return to the car and look south across the fields towards the canal and railway line. During the early stages of the action Goldney sent a party of men under Lieutenant Duncan Nash to hold an eminence of ground which rises slightly to your front about one kilometre distant and then falls to the canal. Nash and his men were almost killed by fire from Neave's Bren gunners in trenches at the south-east corner of Coulogne who could not see over the ridge.

Drive along the **D247** for 300 metres until you reach the junction with the main

The Bridge at Les Attaques where 2/Lieutenant Barr set up his road block.

N43. **Turn right** towards Les Attaques and Ardres. Continue along this fast moving road until you come to a set of traffic lights at the **cross roads in Les Attaques**. **Turn right**. There is a small car park a short distance on the left. Walk to the bridge. It was from here, on the east bank of the canal, at 2 pm on 23 May, that 2/Lieutenant Barr and his men of 'C' Troop 1 Searchlight Regiment opened fire on three German light tanks approaching the bridge from the direction of Guines. Gradually Barr's men were forced back down the street behind you into houses on the other side of the cross-roads. Cross the bridge and walk on for approximately 125 metres until you see the church on your left. Les Attaques Communal Cemetery is approximately 100 metres behind the church to the east and in its south-western corner are the graves of ten British servicemen who fell during the Second World War. Amongst those buried here are Gunner Sidney Pessoll and Bombardier Thomas Tinsley of 1 Searchlight Regiment who were killed in action during the defence of Les Attaques on 23 May.

Retrace your steps across the bridge and back down the street to the cross-roads. You are now following the line of advance of the German medium tanks as

167

Farm Vendroux HQ of C Troop, 1 Searchlight Regiment (2/Lieutenant Barr).

they pushed aside a bus which had blocked their path. At the crossroads two tanks drove straight across and then turned north to outflank Barr's small force, whilst a third turned left and threatened the British barricade on the main road just a few metres away from where you are standing. Eventually Barr's men were surrounded and he surrendered after three hours of continuous fighting. Later that night a patrol of two cruiser and two light tanks of 3RTR under Captain Howe were fired on by anti-tank guns at this spot at around 9.30 pm.

 Return to the car and from the car park drive over the bridge and **turn right** at the 'T' junction just beyond the railway. Follow the road , the **D247E**, which turns sharp left after 800 metres and then sharp right again towards Coulogne. The road crosses level land intersected with many dykes here and after a little over two kilometres **turn right** at the junction and head back towards Coulogne. After 800 metres you will see some farm buildings on your left. This is Farm Vendroux which was the HQ of 2/Lieutenant Barr. It was here at 12.30 pm that a dispatch rider brought news of the German advance towards Les Attaques and with fifty men Barr made his way back along the road you are now on, turned right at the Mairie in Coulogne and hurried past Orphanage Farm on his way to defend the bridge.

 Stay on the road and drive across the level crossing and the bridge over the

Site of Bastion 5 near the Porte de Dunkerque. Note that the moat still exists and follows the line of the earth rampart (now gone).

canal known as the Pont de Briques into the centre of Coulogne. Go straight across the cross-roads in the direction of Calais, passing under the Autoroute after which the road meets the N43 near le Virval. **Turn left** on to the **N43** at the junction and continue for some 700 metres and take the **right turn just before the roundabout** into the Rue de Colmar. You are now following the line of the ramparts and bastions on the eastern face of the outer perimeter which, although much lower than they were in 1940, are nevertheless clearly discernible on the opposite bank of the moat which you can see below you on your left. After 250 metres or so the road bends first right and then left to negotiate the moat around the remains of Bastion 5. Note the German concrete bunker. Here you will reach the junction with the Avenue Antoine de Saint Exupéry at the Porte de Dunkerque. Lieutenant Colonel Ellison-MacCartney moved his HQ into a house near here from Les Fontinettes early on 23 May. Brigadier Nicholson stood at the Dunkirk gate and watched the convoy of 350,000 rations led by Major Hamilton-Russell of 1RB pass through at around 4 am on 24 May. The convoy ran into fierce German resistance at Beau Marais, two kilometres away and had to make a fighting withdrawal.

Turn right and drive along the straight road. On your left you will see the high perimeter wall of the Cimetière Sud, the Calais Southern Cemetery. Parking is available on the road or in one of the side streets on your left. Walk through the main part of the civil cemetery to the south-east corner where you will find the military cemetery, the entrance being marked by the cross of sacrifice. This is the major burial ground for the men of all units killed in action during the battle for Calais, and whose bodies were found and identified, several of whom are mentioned in this guide. Out of the total of 225 graves of the Second World War in plots J to S inclusive, over half that number were killed in action at Calais in the four days between 23 and 26 May 1940 or died later of wounds received between those dates. It is a moving place. 2/Lieutenant Dick Scott, 2KRRC, a great friend of Brigadier Grismond Davies-Scourfield lies here in Plot K Grave 25 as does another 'B' Company officer, Major Henry Scott of Gala in Plot L Grave 3. Davies-Scourfield's trusted Sergeant Henry Wall who steadfastly clung to his isolated post

Calais Southern Cemetery on the Avenue Antoine de Saint Exupery.

near the Place de Norvège until late on 26 May, lies here too. Trooper John Price 3RTR whom Captain Barry O'Sullivan thought was killed in action on 23 May near Hames Boucres lies in Plot M Grave 24.

Return to the car and drive back towards the Porte de Dunkerque. Take the right turn before crossing the bridge over the moat onto the Rue Salvador Allende and continue to the Porte de Marck. At this point it is not possible to continue along the eastern bank of the moat so you must **turn left over the canal** and then **turn right immediately after crossing the bridge**. Note the site of Bastion 4 on your right. You are now driving inside the line of the outer perimeter which was held first by 'A' Company of 2 KRRC and later by 'A' Company of 1RB. **Turn left** at the next junction into the **Rue Mollien** at the Pont de Gravelines and **park the car** as near to the junction as is safe to do so. It was at this spot, thirty or forty metres from the moat and the site of Bastion 3 that Rifleman Douglas Wheeler of 1RB and six other men including PSM Richard 'Sybil' Johnston held a road block during the fighting withdrawal of 'A' Company from the ramparts. There was hand to hand fighting amongst the side streets off the Rue Mollien across the road to the north. From this position PSM Johnston ran down the road towards Bastion 3 with a wheelbarrow to help a wounded man crossing the road. He died in a hail of bullets and his place of burial has never been found. Those like PSM Richard Johnston of 1RB whose bodies were never found or identified are remembered on the panels of the Dunkirk Memorial. Walk east towards Bastion 3. Note the football pitch and school buildings now on the site. Doug Wheeler was captured here at dusk on 25 May attempting to make his way back to the harbour.

Continue down the Rue Mollien towards the town centre after returning to the car and you will eventually cross the Canal de Calais at the Pont Mollien railway bridge. Major Peter Brush, commanding 'I' Company 1RB, received a wound in the throat from a sniper's bullet at this bridge at 8.00 am on the morning of 25 May and refused to seek medical attention until he received a direct order from his commanding officer Lieutenant Colonel Chandos Hoskyns. He resumed command later, was wounded again, but fought on throughout the next day until the last act of the battle when he was taken prisoner fighting alongside riflemen like Don Gurr

Carry on into the **Rue Paul Bert** where you will see the Hotel de Ville on your left and turn right at the roundabout, crossing the Pont Jacquard and the Pont Georges V to return to the tourist office.

Site of Bastion 3. Rifleman Doug Wheeler was captured here on the night of 25 May.

TOURS BY CAR
(to include two walks)

TOUR 3
Beyond the Outer Perimeter to the South. The Tank Action of 3RTR near Hames Boucres. Allow a day

This tour follows in the tracks of the tanks of 3RTR from their assembly areas around Coquelles and Vieux Coquelles to their encounter with the spearhead of Assault Group Kruger of 1 Panzer Divison near the village of Hames Boucres, during the afternoon of 23 May 1940. The initial stage of this tour is by car but the latter stage offers the choice of two circuitous walks around the area of the battlefield. The longer walk of approximately five and half kilometres – which can be extended to just over seven kilometres for those who want to stretch their legs – starts in St. Tricat and follows tracks and footpaths along the line of the advance of the right flank of 3RTR towards the battlefield near Hames Boucres and then returns along the road linking the two villages. The shorter walk of approximately three kilometres starts in Hames Boucres and follows the latter stages of the first walk around the battlefield. For those who prefer not to walk or who would find the tracks difficult to negotiate the battlefield can be viewed from the main roads mentioned in the text without straying too far from the car, although it should be said that some of the tracks and paths on the walk will not accommodate a car of any description.

From the tourist office in the Boulevard Clemenceau **drive towards Pont Georges V and turn right** at the roundabout before crossing the bridge onto the Quai de l'Escaut. At the next roundabout **turn left** and cross the Bassin de la Marne via Pont Freycinet. **Turn right** onto the Avenue Pierre de Coubertin keeping the Citadel and the Cimetière Nord on your right, until you come to the traffic lights. **Turn left** onto the Rue de Verdun and at the next roundabout take the second right sign-posted Coquelles. **Continue** along this straight road passing Fort Nieulay on your right until you come to another roundabout. Go straight across **towards Coquelles**. Drive into **Coquelles and go straight on at the crossroads** in the centre of the

Coquelles. Route de Baron Jean d'Estrees. The old road to Vieux Coquelles and the route taken by some of 3RTR tanks towards Guines.

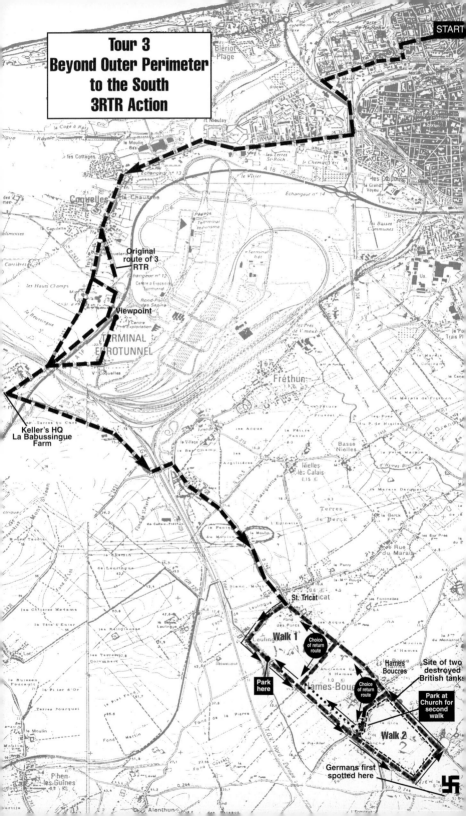

Tour 3
Beyond Outer Perimeter to the South
3RTR Action

START

Original route of 3 RTR

Viewpoint

TERMINAL EUROTUNNEL

Coquelles

Fréthun

Nielles-les-Calais

Keller's HQ La Babussingue Farm

St. Tricat icat

Walk 1

Choice of return route

Park here

Leuline

Hames Boucres

Choice of return route

Site of two destroyed British tanks

Park at Church for second walk

Walk 2

Germans first spotted here

village. The road bends to the left and after approximately 200 metres you will see a road off to your left identified by a 'no through road' sign. This is the Rue de Baron Jean d' Estrees. **Park the car** and walk to the end of the road. At this point the metalled road turns into a narrow track and is blocked by the slip road of junction 12 of the A16 Autoroute. In 1940 this road ran up over the ridge in front of you and down the other side to Vieux Coquelles. This was the route taken by some of the tanks of 3RTR as they moved south to join others from their harbour areas in and around Coquelles and **Vieux Coquelles** en-route to **Guines via St. Tricat** and Hames Boucres. On the other side of the autoroute you can see the vast Cité Europe shopping and leisure complex which has sprung up in conjunction with the opening of the Channel Tunnel.

Return to the car and turn around. At the end of the street **turn left** and climb the hill towards the roundabout easily identified as it has one of the huge boring machines used to carve out the Channel Tunnel as a centrepiece. Take the third exit sign-posted 'Tunnel s/l Manche, Autres Directions A16', and almost immediately you will come to a mini roundabout. Take the **first right** sign-posted 'Vieux Coquelles, Cimetière'. This minor road is the continuation of the old road from Coquelles and passes behind the Château Pigache position which was held by the Germans and fought over during the battles to liberate Calais in September 1944. The Copthorne Hotel now stands on the site.

The road begins to descend and now runs parallel to the A16 but it once ran straight into the old village down the ridge to your left. At the junction at the bottom of the slope **turn left into Vieux Coquelles** and drive under the Autoroute and past the HQ of the Channel Tunnel emergency services on your right. At the next junction in front of the ancient creeper covered church, **turn left** up the hill until you can go no further due to the Autoroute and **park at the top**. Look to the south. On a fine day this is an excellent vantage point from which to view the line of advance of 3RTR which would have approximated the line of the TGV railway you can see snaking out below you to the south-east. In the distance is the ridge line to the south-west of Guines. **Drive back down the slope** to the church and reflect that the tanks would have driven straight on along the track in front of you, a journey denied us today due to the route being barred by the fence protecting the Channel Tunnel rail link which descends into the tunnel just one kilometre on the other side of the Autoroute.

Turn right and pass under the Autoroute until you come to the junction with the D243 E from Coquelles. **Turn left** and after 100 metres or so you will see the entrance and exit to the Channel Tunnel on your right and a short distance after that you will see the white gable end of La Beussingue Farm come into view on your

La Beussingue Farm. First HQ of Colonel Keller CO, 3RTR.

right. This was the first HQ of Lieutenant Colonel Reginald Keller. He was not impressed by the area of Coquelles as a harbour area. Most of the available cover had been taken by French troops and there was little left for his tanks, which he ordered to be dispersed in and around this area as they came off the *Maid of Orleans* in dribs and drabs, such were the problems with unloading.

At the 'T' junction after the farm **turn left** onto the **D215**, sign-posted 'A16, Calais Fréthun, Guines.' Pass over the Autoroute and then drive past a huge red, white and blue Beer and Wine Warehouse on your right until you come to a roundabout. Take the **left turn** and pass under the railway and at the next 'T' Junction **turn right** onto the **D246** to St. Tricat, Hames Boucres and Guines. Note how close the railway is on your right. In 1940 the railway followed the same course and ran almost parallel to the road until it swung south-west across country just before St Tricat to loop around the village of Pihen-les-Guines. Keller's tanks would have been moving in one long column at this point led by an advance guard of three Mark VI light tanks of 'B' Squadron with Sergeant Jimmy Cornwell in the point tank. It had not been possible to get 'C' Squadron out on the right flank 'guard' due to the proximity of the railway.

The road leaves the built up area and the ground starts to undulate with ridges to right and left and 500 metres on the left past the left turn for Nielles de Calais is a farm which was the site of a windmill which Sergeant Jimmy Cornwell remembered as he passed by on his way to Hames Boucres. The road continues over the crest of the ridge and descends into St. Tricat. Take the **second turn** on the right after you enter the village, sign-posted' D245, Pihen-les-Guines' on to the Rue de la Haute Leulingue. You are now following the route of 'C' Squadron under Major Lyons who were able to 'shake out' after passing through the 'bottleneck' of St Tricat as the railway moved westward. Note that the TGV line which passes quite close to the village is a recent addition to the infrastructure of this region. **Continue along the sunken road** until you come to a junction at which you will see a 'Gîtes de France' sign directly opposite. **Turn left** and drive until the road turns sharp right at 90° and the way ahead becomes a farm track. It is just possible to **park off the road** here but the track is used frequently by farm vehicles so do please park with care.

WALK 1 – ST TRICAT, HAMES BOUCRES CIRCUIT

At this point the IGN Series Bleu map shows the long distance footpath called the Tour de Boullonais (GR 120) striking off diagonally across the field to your right but the route shown and the signing of the paths does not always indicate their actual course on the ground. **Walk straight on down the slope along the farm track.** You are now following in the tracks of 'C' Squadron on the right flank of 3RTR's advance across fields and along farm tracks such as this over the undulating countryside. As you descend into the valley between the ridges reflect on the difficulties of observation for tanks in this type of terrain which in 1940 also had more sunken roads than today, and remember that although Keller was probably aware the Germans were moving towards St. Omer he had very little intelligence as to the actual strength or exact location of the German forces in this area. To your left you can see the main road between St. Tricat and Hames Boucres along which the rest of the battalion were moving.

At the cross-tracks in the valley bottom you will see a rock marked with red and

white rectangles. Take the **track indicated by the sign** and walk straight on up the next ridge. As you breast the ridge you will see the buildings of Hames Boucres surrounded by trees and you will come to another cross-tracks. A concrete pole on the floor painted with red and white rectangles indicates the direction of the path. **Go straight on**. To your left front you will see the church steeple of Guines in the distance. You are now descending into Hames Boucres itself and after a short distance you will emerge from between farm buildings onto a metalled road which is the **D231E** the **Rue de l'Église**. **Turn left** and walk 200 metres to the church. On the wall you will see a green and white CWGC sign, and a few metres beyond the gate on the right are the graves of three British soldiers, two Troopers of 3RTR and one unidentified. The men of 3RTR, Trooper Charles Lewis aged twenty-nine and eighteen year old Trooper Thomas Batt, were killed during the battle when two British tanks were destroyed just outside the village on the road to Guines. M. Michel Delplanque and his brother Claude, who still live and farm in the area, remember taking cover in the cellar of their farmhouse on the Rue de Leulingue as children and hearing the noise of the battle raging above and the sound of bullets hitting the roof. They remember clearly the site of the burned out tanks and the burial of the bodies of the troopers. Although the third grave is marked as unknown and the date of death is marked as 24 May, M.

Hames Boucres churchyard. M. Claude Delplanque, who remembers the fighting, stands by the graves of three British soldiers. Two of them belonged to 3RTR killed on the road between Hames Boucres and Guines. The third grave is that of an unidentified soldier.

Claude Delplanque is certain that all three bodies were recovered from the wreckage of the tanks. It is doubtful whether the third body could have been from any unit other than 3RTR given its location, the testimony of local people and the fact that it lies next to two identified bodies.

   Retrace your steps to the junction with the footpath. This is the road along which Major Simpson commanding 'A' Squadron got his tanks along and into action after being called forward from St. Tricat by Keller after 'B' Squadron had confirmed contact with the Germans. **Turn left** into the Rue de Leulingue and walk on. Major Simpson would have pushed some of his tanks across the open fields in the direction in which you are walking. The first farm on your left belongs to M. Michel Delplanque. At the point where the road starts to bend to the right take the footpath which forks **to the left** which is clearly signposted 'Sentier l'Hermitage'. Walk to the top of the ridge. This is a superb spot from which to view the battlefield of 23 May. To your left surrounded by trees are the buildings of La Waille Farm which, in 1940, was called Grand St Blaise. Notice how the ground slopes down to the farm and the road to your right (D244). The buildings in front of you are those of le Grand St. Blaise Château and St. Blaise Farm which were unnamed on Keller's maps. Major Reeves reported that his advance guard passed through Hames Boucres and

175

Scene of the 3RTR tank action 23 May 1940. C Squadron's eye view of the battlefield looking south from the footpath towards German positions in front of the line of trees and outbuildings of Grand St Blaise Château. The spires of Guines can be seen to the left.

crested the ridge on the south side of the village and both Sergeant Jimmy Cornwell and Captain Barry O' Sullivan saw movements about 1000 metres to their right front from a position on the main road just outside Hames Boucres behind you and to your left. Walk on down the ridge and imagine yourself in a tank moving slowly down the slope in murky conditions and running into the vehicles of a German armoured column resting along the road to your right and on the track in front of the farm buildings in front of you. Note how the ground rises and falls away gently towards the buildings in front and reflect on the fact that Major Quentin Carpendale got to within twenty metres of the Germans before they realized his was a British tank. A German officer, who was probably as surprised as Carpendale to see a British tank moving towards him, fired a revolver at Carpendale who turned and raced back up the slope.

After 300 metres or so you will see another signpost which will direct you on a path **to your left** leading to the main road at La Waille Farm. After the initial encounter the battle developed in the fields all around you in the triangle of land bounded by the D244 road to your right the D 215 main road to your left and the D231 E road between Hames Boucres and the junction with the D244 with the British advancing and firing and the Germans replying with anti-tank guns and later with a field gun. At first the British cruisers with their two pounders held their own but the appearance of the German field artillery and accurate anti-tank fire swung the balance in favour of the Germans and Keller ordered a retirement. Walk along the path heading north-east. To your left you can see quite clearly the ridge over which some of the British tanks advanced and then withdrew back towards Hames Boucres.

At the junction of the path and the main road **turn left** on to the main road and walk back towards Hames Boucres. Take care on this stretch of road as there is not much by way of a verge and the traffic tends to speed along to and from Guines. After approximately 750 metres, just before you reach the buildings of the village,

you will come to the spot where the two British tanks were destroyed and from which came the bodies of the troopers buried in Hames Boucres churchyard were recovered. The burned out hulks lay at this spot until 1941 when they were finally removed.

See page 73

After entering the village you have the choice of turning left on to the D 231 E2 sign-posted 'Caffiers, Pihen-les-Guines, Marquise' or walking straight on up the hill along the main road to St Tricat. The former will take you in the tracks of Major Simpson's tanks at the start of the battle as far as the footpath opposite the Rue de Leulingue and from there you can retrace your steps back over the undulating ground to the car near St Tricat much as Keller's tanks did during their withdrawal to a ridge south of Coquelles during the late afternoon of 23 May.

The latter option will also take you up and over the ridge to the north of Hames Boucres and into the bottom of the valley before the road begins to climb again to St Tricat, take the farm track known as the Fond d'Hames. This track leads back to the cross-tracks at the bottom of the slope at the top of which the car is parked. If you want to extend your walk carry on along the road until you enter St.Tricat and turn left onto the D245 and then left again after 750 metres and return to the car.

If you decide to walk down the Fond d'Hames look straight ahead and beyond the TGV railway is the old railway line behind which Keller thought he would retire and re-group for another attack. This was not to be and he later ordered a more general retirement towards Calais. At the junction of the paths turn right and head back up the slope towards the car.

WALK 2 – HAMES BOUCRES CIRCUIT

For a shorter walk around Hames Boucres only, drive straight through St Tricat to Hames Boucres. In the village take the second major turn on your right onto the D 231 E2 sign-posted 'Caffiers, Pihen-les-Guines, Marquise, Église Mairie,' and drive for 800 metres until you see the church on the right. It is possible to park the car on the left, just before the church. You can begin the walk by visiting the graves

177

German positions

The road from Hames Boucres to Guines. The vehicles mark the site where the two British tanks were destroyed. British eye view of the battlefield. See page 73.

of the two troopers of 3RTR killed in action on 23 May 1940, and the grave of one unidentified serviceman as mentioned earlier. From the churchyard the route of the shorter walk follows that of the longer walk described in detail above; returning to the car parked at the church by taking the D231 E2 in the centre of Hames Boucres.

Returning to Calais via the Coquelles Ridge

After returning to the car **drive back to La Beussingue Farm** and turn onto the **D 243E** towards Coquelles up the slopes of the ridge. Ahead of you on the skyline you will see the old wooden windmill on top of the Coquelles Ridge which was also a landmark for many men of 3RTR. At the crest of the ridge on your right you will see the entrance to the Copthorne Hotel. Continue for another twenty metres or so and park the car. Walk downhill towards the roundabout where the boring machine stands until you have passed the last house on your right and look to the north-east. Lieutenant Colonel Keller's tanks would have made this journey down the ridge as they withdrew into Calais at around 9 pm on the night of 23 May after their encounter with 1 Panzer Division. Major Reeves had already witnessed German columns of another Panzer Division the 10th, wending their way towards Calais that evening. They occupied the ridge during the night. The view you see is similar to that of the German soldiers and artillery men at dawn on 24 May after they had moved their guns on to the Coquelles ridge. The advantages of the ridge for observation are immediately obvious as the Hôtel de Ville, the lighthouse and the derricks of the cranes on the docks stand out just as much today as they did in 1940, providing excellent reference points upon which the German gunners could register their targets. It was from this ridge that the German infantry of 86 Rifle Regiment launched their assault on Fort Nieulay and the western and south-western faces of the outer perimeter at 5 am on the morning of 24 May.

Return to the car and drive straight across at the roundabout into Coquelles, returning to the tourist office in Calais by reversing the route taken at the beginning of the tour.

178

TOUR 4

The Inner Perimeter of Calais-Nord. A Walk Around Some of the Key Points in the Defence of the Old Town

Allow a Day to Complete the Whole Walk

From the tourist office on the Boulevard Clemenceau walk south towards **Pont Georges V**. In 1940 this bridge was known as Pont Richelieu and was the centre of the three bridges held by 'D' Company of 2KRRC under Lord Godfrey Cromwell on 25 and 26 May. The bridge has undergone extensive reconstruction since 1940. It was at this bridge, at 11 am on Saturday 25 May, that Andre Gershell, the Mayor of Calais, arrived in a German armoured car with a surrender demand for Brigadier Nicholson from General Schall, commanding 10 Panzer Division. Here also, four hours later at 3pm the same day, Leutnant Hoffman of the German 69 Rifle Regiment arrived on the same errand. Both requests were refused point blank by Nicholson. His written reply to the surrender demands brought by Hoffman was written down in English in the 10 Panzer Division War Diary.

Continue south and **cross the Pont Jacquard** with the central railway station on your right and walk straight on at the roundabout. On your left you will see the red brick edifice of the Hôtel de Ville. Note the clock tower which provided an excellent platform for German observers and snipers after the Hôtel de Ville was occupied at 8.00 am on the morning of 25 May. From that vantage point German marksmen and artillery observers could overlook the whole of the Old Town of Calais-Nord including the key areas around all the approaches to the three bridges vital for the defence of the inner perimeter, Freycinet, Richelieu and Faidherbe, all of which 2KRRC had blocked with vehicles. It was outside the Hôtel de Ville that a patrol led by Major Peter Brush, commanding 'I' Company 1RB, fired on German officers lining civilians up for interrogation just after 7 am on the morning of 25 May. Note also the famous sculpture of the Six Burghers of Calais by Rodin which, before the battle, stood on

Pont Georges V. The centre of the three bridges connecting Calais Nord to Calais St Pierre. German snipers in the tower of the Hôtel de Ville overlooked the barricades and postions of the defenders.

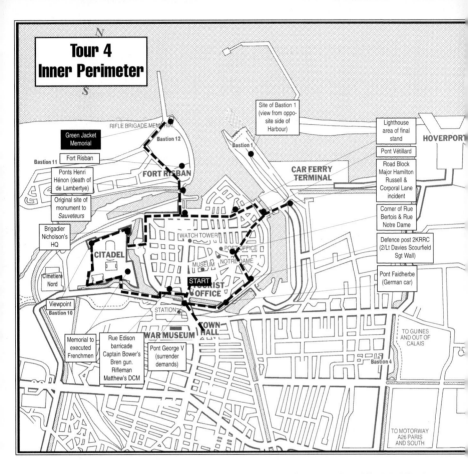

Tour 4
Inner Perimeter

a plinth near the Parc Richelieu and was placed in the crypt of the Hôtel de Ville for safe keeping after the German invasion of the Low Countries and Northern France on 10 May. After this date many Calais schoolgirls had their lessons around the base of the statue as they sheltered from air raids in the crypt.

Walk across the road into the Parc St. Pierre. This is where the transport of 'B' Echelon of 3RTR was parked after the battalion's arrival in Calais on 22 May. Sergeant Bill Close, whose Daimler Dingo reconnaissance car was used by Brigadier Nicholson as a 'battle taxi', remembers the flower beds and paths being littered with shards of broken glass from the greenhouses which used to stand in the park. Visit the **Calais War Museum** which is housed in twenty rooms in a concrete blockhouse almost in the middle of the park. The ninety-four metre long ferro-concrete construction called the 'Mako' bunker was built by the Germans as a central telephone exchange and HQ of the Port Commandant during the occupation. Among the exhibits is a section devoted to the Green Jackets who, hopelessly out-numbered and out-gunned, fought alongside the 800 French 'Volunteers of Calais' to the bitter end. The museum has access for wheelchair users and is open every day from 10.00 am until 6.00 pm with a last admission at 5.15 pm during the period 1 April to 30 September. From 1 February until 31 March

180

and again between 1 October and 30 November the museum is open from 11am until 5.00 pm with the last admission at 4.15 pm, but it is closed on Tuesdays. It was closed completely during the December of 1998 and January of 1999. It would be advisable to check with the tourist office on current admission charges and opening times to avoid disappointment.

From the Parc St. Pierre **retrace your steps** and **re-cross Pont Georges V. Turn left** immediately after the bridge and walk west along the Quai de l'Escaut. Riflemen of 'D' Company 2KRRC had broken into the original houses which stood along this road to your right and had made them into defensive positions covering the far bank of the Bassin de la Marne to your left. Walk on until you reach the Pont Freycinet, the 'right' of the three bridges defended by 2KRRC. **Cross the road** and walk towards the corner of the **Quai de l'Escaut and Rue Edison**. It was across the end of this street (nearest the bridge) that 2KRRC had built a road block. It was at this very spot that Captain Claude Bower fell mortally wounded whilst firing a Bren gun from underneath a truck at around 10.15 am on the morning of 26 May as the Germans concentrated their fire on the barricade. Such was the continuous stream of machine-gun bullets that stretcher bearers were unable to attend to Captain Bower or any of the other wounded Riflemen. Rifleman Matthews of 2KRRC earned the DCM when he backed a truck up towards the barricade amid a torrent of bullets to recover Captain Bower, but finding him already dead he succeeded in removing several more of his wounded comrades and drove them to safety. Here also Rifleman Eric Chambers witnessed the bizarre incident when Captain Bower's Bren gun suddenly started firing as German infantry made their way across the bridge, even though Rifleman Matthews had found Bower to be dead.

Walk south towards the bridge Pont Freycinet. You are now following in the footsteps of Captain Stanton who, shortly after 7.30 pm on 25 May, whilst in temporary command of 'A' Company 2KRRC, led a counter-attack against a German tank which had forced the road-block on the bridge supported by infantry of 86 Rifle Regiment. The tank was driven back but a few German soldiers succeeded in taking up positions in some of the houses towards the Citadel to your right. During the assault Captain Stanton was hit several times in the body but

Defenders' view looking across Pont Freycinet canal bridge.

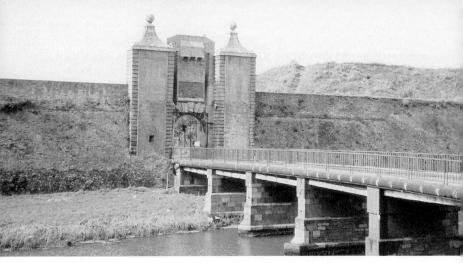

The Neptune Gate leading into the Citadel. See page 28.

staggered back to report to his commanding officer, Lieutenant Colonel Euan Miller at whose feet he collapsed and died.

Cross the bridge and walk further west along the Avenue Pierre de Coubertin towards the Citadel and **enter by the Boulogne or South Gate**. You will be following in the tracks of the German infantrymen of 86 Rifle Regiment who forced their way into the stronghold at around 4.30 pm on the afternoon of Sunday 26 May. Note the memorial plaque to the dead of the KRRC, the RB and QVR on the wall of the inner gate. Once inside and to the right, there is a memorial stone to five young Frenchmen who were shot on that spot at dawn on 3 September 1944, just twenty-seven days before the liberation of Calais. They had been imprisoned in the Citadel for attempting an act of sabotage in the factory where they worked.

A walk around the ramparts of the Citadel, which is now a sports stadium, will reveal its great strength, although the ramparts are somewhat overgrown today and are used as a trim track by joggers. As you stroll around the Citadel imagine what it must have been like sixty years ago, with Stuka dive-bombers screaming down through smoke filled skies to drop load after load of explosive and incendiary bombs

View from the north west bastion of the Citadel looking towards Bastion 11 where the apartment block now stands.

Site of Bastion 11

onto Brigadier Nicholson, Colonel Holland and the mixed force of British and French defenders sheltering in the vaulted tunnels under the ramparts and bastions. It was in the north-east corner of the Citadel that Brigadier Nicholson had his HQ during the latter stages of the battle. Note the brick entrances leading to the tunnels. Brigadier Nicholson was taken prisoner just after 4.30 pm that Sunday afternoon along with Colonel Holland and his Brigade Major Dennis Talbot who later managed to slip away from a column of marching prisoners and escaped back across the Channel to England. It was somewhere on the site of the present day football pitch that Brigadier Nicholson received Andre Gershell the Mayor of Calais, who had brought the first of General Schall's surrender demands at around 9.00 am on 25 May. It was refused as was Hoffman's later that day. From the top of the north-western ramparts look north-west towards the coast and you will see the apartment blocks and the Aqua'rile restaurant on top of Bastion 11. It is clear from this position how close Bastion 11 was to the Citadel and how its fall enabled the Germans to put pressure on Bastion 12 and Fort Risban – which you can see if you look east towards the harbour – and eventually the Citadel itself.

Leave the Citadel by the East or Neptune Gate but before you pass through the outer gate reflect on the fact that the area between the inner and outer gates, was the first place of burial of several officers and riflemen of 1 RB and 2 KRRC killed in action at Calais, including Captain Claude Bower, 2/Lieutenant Dick Scott and 2/Lieutenant Adrian Van de Weyer. Several of the bodies could not be positively identified due to extensive burns, but one found with £40 or £50 sterling in his battledress was believed to have been Major Owen 2i/c 2KRRC. Once you have crossed the moat and emerged on the main road **turn left** and head north along the Rue Jaques Vendroux until the road bears right at a roundabout and becomes the Boulevard de la Résistance. Walk east until you come to the **two bridges** which cross the Bassin Ouest and the Bassin des Chasses, which are known as the Ponts Henri Hénon. Walk across the bridges and as you do so recall that it was at some point on one of the bridges that the French naval commander, Carlos de Lambertye, suffered a heart attack and died in the heat of battle after bolstering some French marines who had become nervous due to the ferocity of the German onslaught. Fort Risban, which was de Lambertye's HQ and was his destination at the time he collapsed on the Ponts Henri Hénon, is on the other side of the bridges and in 1940 was held by French troops. It used to be possible to walk around the earth ramparts and to see the grass covered depressions caused by the German and later the Allied bombardments, as well as a series of tunnels at ground level and the remains of a chapel built in the 17th century at the time of Vauban. At the time of writing, however, the fort was closed to the public and only members of the yacht club which has its club house on the quay in front of the fort, were allowed access. That said, there is talk of refurbishing the fort and opening it up to the public once more but as yet no firm plans have been laid.

Walk on past Fort Risban along the Avenue Raymond Poincare towards the beach. On your right you will pass signs for a camp site which now stands on the site of Bastion 12, also held by the French during the battle. A little further on you will see signs indicating parking on your right. Follow the signs and walk through the car park towards the quay-side at the western entrance to the harbour. You will soon see the cross of sacrifice marking the site of the Green Jacket War memorial which was moved from its original position on the site of the last stand of 1RB at Bastion 1 in 1998 and re-dedicated at a ceremony which took place on 20 May of that year. During that ceremony, forty-seven Calais veterans paraded under the command of

The Green Jacket memorial moved from the site of Bastion 1 and re-dedicated 20 May 1998.

Brigadier Grismond Davies-Scourfield, who as a 2/Lieutenant with 2 KRRC, had fought throughout the battle until he was wounded three times and captured on 26 May, 1940.

Look south-east across the harbour towards the ferry terminal. The unusual, angular shape of the Capitainerie, the harbour master's office, you see in front of you, marks the site of the final struggle of the Rifle Brigade on that Sunday afternoon. As you can see, nothing now remains of the mound which was Bastion 1 or the tunnel beneath it in which so many wounded men sheltered from the German artillery shells and the bombs of the Stukas due to the development of the ferry terminal in the late 1990's. It was in a trench near the site of the Capitainerie that Lieutenant Colonel Chandos Hoskyns, commanding 1RB, received a fatal wound from a shell splinter. On that quay also was the Gare Maritime which was destroyed during the battle and has long since disappeared.

Retrace your steps and re-cross the Ponts Henri Hénon until you reach the Boulevard des Alliés. It was here that the monument to the lifeboat crews, the

The Quai Crespin, buildings that survived the fighting, now the Calais Chamber of Commerce. See p.136

'Sauveteurs' of Calais, stood throughout the battle and miraculously escaped destruction when many of the buildings around it were completely gutted. The monument now stands on the Quai Delpierre. **Turn left** and walk east along the Boulevard towards the area around the lighthouse, the Phare de Calais. It was in this district during Sunday afternoon, 26 May, that the German infantry and panzers hunted out isolated parties of 2KRRC and 1QVR who had not surrendered or received the 'every man for himself' message issued by Lieutenant Colonel Miller. It is possible to visit the lighthouse which offers a superb view of the Old Town from the platform below the lamp room. The hours of opening between 1 June and 30 September are from 10 am until noon and then again from 2pm until 6.30 pm at week-ends and from 2pm until 6.30 pm during the week. Between 1 October and 31 May, week-end openings are from 10 am until 12 noon and then again from 2 pm until 5 pm, whilst during the week it opens from 2 pm until 5.30 pm. The number of visitors is limited so do check with the tourist office if you are part of a large group.

From the lighthouse **continue** to walk along the Boulevard des Alliés until it opens up into the cobbled area criss-crossed by railway lines, known as the Place de l'Europe. Walk **towards the bridge** and lock known as the Pont Vétillard and the Écluse Carnot. It was this bridge which 2/Lieutenant The Right Honourable Terrence Prittie, 1RB, tried to destroy with anti-tank mines on the evening of 24th May, without success. Also in this area, a short distance to your left along the Quai Paul Devot, Rifleman Thomas Sandford of 2KRRC made his last stand defending the lock gates with a few comrades and was taken prisoner after a stick grenade had blown him off his feet. A German officer drew a knife on Sandford but only cut off the Rifleman's respirator much to Sandford's relief.

Just across the bridge and 200 metres to the right on the corner of the Quai du Rhône and the Quai de la Loire was the site of a road block and barricade of 1RB held by Major Arthur 'Boy' Hamilton Russell. It was from there that a party of seventeen men under the command of Major Brush launched a counter attack at 3.30 pm on Saturday 25 May but were held up almost immediately by heavy fire. Here also, Corporal Lane arrived in a truck filled with wounded men along the Quai de la Loire from the direction of the advancing Germans with a gun pressed to the head of the driver who was a suspected 'Fifth Columnist'. 2/Lieutenant Edward Bird was killed here as he tried to restart the truck which had been hit and Major Brush and his men pulled the wounded from the blazing vehicle before retiring back towards the site of the present day Capitainerie.

From the bridge head back towards town and walk along the street ahead called the Rue Lamy which leads into the Place de Suede. **Take the second street on your left**, the Rue de Londres and walk until the road opens out into a grass covered square set with lines of trees called the Place d' Angleterre. **Turn right** and walk past the entrance to the Rue de Madrid until you come to the corner of Rue Berthois and Rue Notre Dame and look along the Rue Notre Dame. This road runs past the church from which it takes its name all the way to the Place d'Armes and it was along this road that 2KRRC were ordered to take up a final string of posts from the Boulevard des Alliés near the Ponts Henri Hénon to the Place d'Angleterre as the Germans advanced across the bridges during the early afternoon of 26 May.

Turn around and **retrace your steps** to the Place d'Angleterre and turn right when you reach the square. Walk to the south-west corner of the square and note the proximity and the dominating position of the clock tower of the Hôtel de Ville as you look straight down the Rue de Bruxelles. Walk a short distance to the east to the junction with the Rue de Hollande It was near this spot, in the cellars of two

Place d'Anglettere looking along Rue Bruxelles towards Pont Faidherbe. B Coy 2KRRC HQ was in a house near where the white van is parked.

houses on the corner of the Place d'Angleterre and the Rue Hollande that Major Jack Poole, commanding 'B' Company 2KRRC, set up his HQ after withdrawing from the outer perimeter during the night of 24/25 May and it was here that both Major Henry Scott and 2/Lieutenant Dick Scott were killed, the latter shot by a sniper as he crossed the street with a message from Lieutenant Colonel Miller. Corporal Ron Savage was taken prisoner near here when German tanks entered the square from the right and the left as he and four of his comrades sheltered in a doorway from withering fire.

Walk south along the Rue Hollande until it opens up into a rather featureless

Looking along Rue Notre Dame towards Place d'Armes and the Tour Guet. A line of defensive positions was established along this street by 2KRRC.

Place d'Anglettere looking along Rue de Hollande towards Place de Norvège. The continuation of the line of defensive positions linking up Place d'Armes with Place de Norvège. Corporal Savage's section, 5 Platoon, B Coy, made a break from their house down this street but were surrounded by German tanks entering the square from the east and the west.

'circus' called the Place de Norvège. In a house on the corner of the Place de Norvège and the Quai de la Volga 2/Lieutenant Grismond Davies-Scourfield, commanding 5 platoon, 2KRRC, set up a defensive post under Sergeant Wall, who was killed on 26 May. Looking south, note the proximity of the bridge and the waterway and reflect on the fact that this became a front line position on the 25 May as 1RB withdrew north along the Quai de la Loire to your left, and it remained so

View east along Quai de la Volga from the Place de Norvège. 2/Lieutenant Davies-Scourfield, B Coy, 2 KRRC, was wounded here and managed to crawl to a hut on the quayside where he was discovered by a lone German soldier.

throughout 26 May. It was in this vicinity that Davies-Scourfield set out to rally his isolated posts and strayed too close to the canal bank at around 4 pm on 26 May. He came under fire from the far bank of the canal in front of you and was hit in the right arm, the side and the head. He crawled to a hut nearby on the quay-side and was found by a lone German after the fighting had died down.

From the Place de Norvège walk west along the waterfront on the Quai de la Meuse towards the 'left' of the three bridges known as Pont Faidherbe. Here, at 1 am on Sunday 26 May, Corporal Humby and Rifleman Ewings of 2KRRC, crawled across the bridge to search a German staff car which had attempted to cross behind tanks the previous evening, during which attack their second in command, Major Oswald 'Puffin' Segar-Owen, was killed. Their journey across the bridge and back again took two hours.

Continue to walk along the waterfront on the Quai de la Tamise. Note the houses along the road. These have been completely rebuilt along with 95% of the rest of the Old Town of Calais-Nord. It was from the original buildings running parallel to the canal that 'D' Company 2KRRC fired on the Germans as they did along the Quai de l'Escaut further west.

Turn right when you reach Pont Georges V and complete the tour by returning to the tourist office on the Boulevard Clemenceau.

View from Pont Faidherbe towards Hôtel de Ville. British rifleman's eye view from the road block on the bridge.

SELECT BIBLIOGRAPHY

Borchert, H. *Panzerkampf im Westen* (Berlin 1940)

Close, Major B. *A View From the Turret* (Dell & Bredon 1998)

Davies-Scourfield, G. *In Presence of My Foes* (Wilton 65 1991)

Ellis, L.F. T*he War in France & Flanders, 1939-40* (HMSO, 1953)

Glover, M. *The Fight for the Channel Ports* (Leo Cooper, 1985)

Guderian, Generaloberst (Ed.) *Mit den Panzern in Ost und West* vol.i (Berlin 1942)

Harding, W. *A Cockney Soldier* (Merlin 1989)

Hastings, Major R.H.W.S. *The Rifle Brigade in the Second World War 1939-1945* (Gale & Polden, 1950)

Lyme, E. *Soldier in the Circus* (The Book Guild 1997)

Mills, Brigadier G. H. & Nixon, Lt. Col. R. F. *The Annals of the King's Royal Rifle Corps* vol. vi. 1921-1943 (Leo Cooper, 1971)

Neave, A. *The Flames of Calais* (Hodder & Stoughton, 1972)

Parkyn, Major H.G. (Ed) *The Rifle Brigade Chronicle 1945* (Gale &Polden, 1946)

The King's Royal Rifle Corps Chronicle 1940 (Warren & Son Ltd., 1941)

Wake, Major-Gen Sir H. & Deedes, Major W.F. *Swift and Bold: The King's Royal Rifle Corps in the Second World War* (Gale & Polden, 1949)

INDEX